Teaching
Beginner ELLs
Using Picture Books

Teaching **Beginner ELLs** Using Picture Books

Tellability

ANA LADO

CORWIN
A SAGE Company

FOR INFORMATION:

Corwin

A SAGE Company

2455 Teller Road

Thousand Oaks, California 91320

(800) 233-9936

www.corwin.com

SAGE Publications Ltd.

1 Oliver's Yard

55 City Road

London EC1Y 1SP

United Kingdom

SAGE Publications India Pvt. Ltd.

B 1/I 1 Mohan Cooperative Industrial Area

Mathura Road, New Delhi 110 044

India

SAGE Publications Asia-Pacific Pte. Ltd.

3 Church Street

#10-04 Samsung Hub

Singapore 049483

Acquisitions Editor: Dan Alpert

Associate Editor: Megan Bedell

Editorial Assistant: Sarah Bartlett

Production Editor: Cassandra Margaret Seibel

Copy Editor: Cate Huisman

Typesetter: C&M Digitals (P) Ltd.

Proofreader: Caryne Brown

Indexer: Jean Casalegno

Cover Designer: Gail Buschman

Permissions Editor: Karen Ehrmann

Printed in the United States of America.

Library of Congress Cataloging-in-Publication Data

Lado, Ana.
Teaching beginner ELLs using picture books : tellability / Ana Lado.

p. cm.
Includes bibliographical references and index.

ISBN 978-1-4522-3523-3 (pbk.)

1. English language—Study and teaching—Foreign speakers. 2. Second language acquisition. 3. Picture books—Study and teaching. 4. Language experience approach in education. I. Title.

PE1128.A2L235 2012
428.0071—dc23   2012020408

This book is printed on acid-free paper.

12 13 14 15 16 10 9 8 7 6 5 4 3 2 1

Contents

Glossary of Acronyms

CLT Communicative Language Teaching
ELL English Language Learner
ELP English Language Proficiency
LEA Language Experience Approach (a teaching strategy)
TESOL Teaching English to Speakers of Other Languages
TPR Total Physical Response (a teaching strategy)

Additional materials and resources related to *Teaching Beginner ELLs Using Picture Books: Tellability* can be found at http://www.corwin.com/picturebooks4ells.

Preface

Writing this book reminded me of my first piano lessons. I was a true beginner. My teacher, Mr. Bader, began with simple tunes requiring only the use of my right hand. Gradually, and thankfully, he incorporated the left hand and an ever-expanding repertoire of notes. I use a similar graduated approach when teaching English to beginner *English language learners* (ELLs). I begin with simple picture books that optimize language learning. As ELLs progress, I incorporate books that require increased amounts of English communicative competency. This graduated approach improves the pace of their English development.

Picture books convey meaning through visual media just as much as through text (Benedict & Carlisle, 1992; Wolfenbarger & Sipe, 2007). Their visuals are more than just the illustrations accompanying text. They have a variety of graphic elements, such as special fonts, graphic organizers, and illustrated glossaries.

Picture books also convey meaning socially. This is sometimes the result of spontaneous sharing when a book is read aloud. It is often the result of purposely embedded interactive elements, such as flaps for readers to lift or questions for them to answer. Visual images and verbal text are static; the pictures and text do not change. In comparison, socially mediated meaning is fluid, because it reflects the participants and situation. Authors and illustrators creatively exploit distinct elements in all three media (Galda, Culllihan, & Sipe, 2010; Nikolajeva & Scott, 2006; Sipe, 2008). Taken as a whole, picture books are a multidimensional medium that is a rich resource for a broad range of instructional situations.

It is true that many picture books assume a young audience of native speakers of English. It is easy to find books for this audience and less so for other types of students. However, it is also true that there are a good number of picture books that appeal to readers of all ages, levels of artistic sophistication, background languages, and ranges of reading abilities (Anstey, 2002; Hall, 2007; Lott, 2001; Tiedt & Tiedt, 2005). There are simply lots of books covering an array of subjects and styles, making it possible to accommodate each student across K–12 curriculum areas. Teachers in search of the right book for a particular class need only consult one of the many resources available, such as the annotated book lists with information about reading levels or curriculum connections.

The types of books used with ELLs have features compatible with the students' linguistic abilities. Picture books with the following qualities are particularly well suited to second language instruction: universal themes, easy-to-access sparse text, clarifying illustrations, and formats associated with language-learning activities. For example, a repetitive format lends itself to oral fluency practice. Book lists for ELLs categorize picture books using standard descriptions of *English language proficiency* (ELP). These standards divide the ELP continuum into broadly defined levels for the purpose of placing ELLs into a program. This way the needs of ELLs in different levels are accommodated with appropriately differentiated instructional content, teaching strategies, and materials.

However, within the beginner level there is a wide range of abilities. The earliest beginner can access English only when provided with a maximum of scaffolds to meaning. Typically, language teachers help these students by using a maximum of pictures, gestures, and objects. With later beginners, they use fewer scaffolds. Picture books listed as being at a beginner level range in the amount of scaffolds they contain. Thus, a book found on a list may be just right for the later-stage beginner and yet overwhelm the earliest-stage student. Even among the earliest beginners, the need for books with embedded scaffolds differs, because they come to the task with a wide range of characteristics, such as their first language, age, and educational background.

We need lists of books that help identify a book's usefulness for teaching different types of beginner ELLs. Few picture book lists contain this type of detail about a book's linguistic and nonlinguistic scaffolds. Few provide specific information about the topic, text, illustrations, and formats for matching books to particular types of beginning ELLs. One of the reasons for this lack of detail is probably that situational variables are complex and difficult to codify.

Picture books are experienced and read in many ways. Teachers adapt their reading to the situation and students, and in doing so significantly reduce a book's difficulty. For example, a wordless picture book in one situation is a barrier to learning English, because there is no written text for ELLs to use as a model. In another situation, an English-speaking teacher finds this same book ideal, because it requires students only to use the oral language they know, rather than being challenged by language beyond their ability. In this example, the utility of the same book is low in one situation and high in the other. Even though these types of situational variables are complex and flexible, they are worth including on book lists for beginner ELLs.

We can start the process by selecting picture books based on the principles of *communicative language teaching* (CLT). These are grounded in second language learning and acquisition research.[1] We use these to select materials that reflect the teaching of communicative competence in English (Canale, 1983; Uso-Juan & Martinez-Flor, 2006). Communicative competency requires ELLs to develop linguistic, discourse, strategic, and sociocultural abilities. It applies to our goal of developing the ELLs' ability to know what, when, where, and how to use language. CLT principles apply to beginning instruction in a picture book context. They are a springboard for developing English ability in other contexts.

I refer to picture books that are compatible with teaching ELL beginners as books with *tellability*.[2] This term helps focus attention on our goal of teaching ELLs *communicative competency*, a broader ability than just reading or linguistic skills. There are enormous benefits to using books with tellability. Finding these books requires categorizing beginner books into narrower ranges of ELP within the broadly defined beginner level. It also requires weaving together several criteria. I find books with tellability by applying a few steps.

Basically, I look for books that favor language development through scaffolds, themes, language difficulty, and format. As you read this book, you will recognize standard criteria for selecting books, such as using concrete topics and repetitive language. However, you will also come across some criteria that will be new to you, such as using book features compatible with specific CLT strategies.

CRITERIA FOR PICTURE BOOK SELECTION

Beginner ELLs are overwhelmed with the large amounts of unfamiliar language, themes, and formats contained in many picture books. The written text is "too dense a linguistic package for language learning purposes" (Rost, 2006, p. 51). Even a book with few words can be confusing to an ELL, because these words are sophisticated and abstract and are presented in complex syntactic structures. The book should contain scaffolds promoting English development (Cox & Boyd-Batstone, 2009). I use the following four overarching categories to find picture books with tellability:

1. **Communicative Language Teaching:** My book selection is grounded in the basic principles governing the teaching of a second language (Curtain & Dahlberg, 2010; Ellis, 2008; Lado, 1988; Long, 1990a; Nation, 2001).

Nation sums up these four strands of a balanced CLT program as meaningful comprehensible input, expressive output, language-focused learning, and fluency.

2. **Topic:** I select books thematically. Themes accelerate language-learning by providing repetition of words and structures and build background knowledge to ease ELLs into participation (Grabe & Stroller, 2001; Rost, 2006). The themes shown below are popular ones in picture books with sparse text. For each theme, there are at least a dozen sparse-text books that are appropriate for school-aged ELLs. These themes are:

- Animals. There are so many picture books about animals that it is possible to create subthemes, such as butterflies, farm animals, tiny animals, and pets. An overwhelming majority of books about pets are about cats and dogs. The tiny animal subtheme includes bugs, insects, spiders, worms, and any small animals, as most picture books do not use scientific classifications.
- Concepts. There are many picture books about basic concepts taught to beginner ELLs, such as the names of letters, items of clothing, and colors.
- Crafts and art.
- Food.
- Fiction and language arts.
- Friendship. I include in this theme animal allegories about cooperation, tolerance, and friendships.
- Humor.
- Mathematics. An overwhelming number of picture books are about the subtheme of counting and numbers. Other subthemes include measurement and shapes.
- Music. This theme includes folklore and songs.
- People. This theme includes books about celebrations in the United States and around the world. A good number of the people-themed books are about families and are annotated as such.
- Science. This theme includes books about nature, plants, and space.
- Social studies. This theme includes geography, biography, autobiography, and culture.
- Time. Included in this theme are books about the weather, seasons, days of the week, and months.
- Transportation. This theme includes books dealing with vehicles and travel.

3. **Language Difficulty:** I select books within the beginner ELP level. Most of these books can be further categorized into four stages of beginner

difficulty. However, some types of picture books are not easy to place into one of these four stages. When it is impractical to categorize a book into one of the four stages, I label it according to its format. These format categories are *poem, song, multistage, wordless,* and *picture dictionary.*

4. **Communicative Language Teaching Strategies:** I list books by their compatibility with a CLT strategy. For example, a book that features active verbs is easy to use with total physical response (TPR). The CLT strategies I selected represent a balance of comprehension, expression, language-focused learning, and fluency and are compatible with features commonly found in sparse-text picture books. The 12 CLT strategies are as follows:

- Chanting and singing. Books for expressive language development and fluency practice, such as texts with a singsong repetitive style and texts that are short enough to be reread. Books for singing require lyrics and musical scores or audio recordings.
- Compare and contrast. Books with parallel information, versions in different languages, or comparable features for graphing the text.
- Graphics. Books with graphic items like maps, matrixes, diagrams, and other graphic presentations of concepts for language-focused text graphing.
- Guessing games. Concept books with question-and-answer formats or information gaps for inquiring, identifying, describing, and analyzing ideas.
- Language experience approach (LEA). Project-based books for teaching the language of project directives, procedures, recipes, and crafts.
- Model-based writing. Books containing literary devices or templates for guiding written expression, such as books written as a diary or letter.
- Reader's theater. Books with text to read aloud for improving fluency, such as oral-style text, first person accounts, and dialogue.
- Realia. Stories for teaching comprehension that contain salient objects or embedded textures. *Realia* is the CLT term for objects, artifacts, and models.
- Recitation. Books that each contain a single poem that students can recite to improve oral fluency and interpretation.
- Retelling. Books with transparently written or illustrated sequential stories for teaching expression, paraphrasing, and summarizing.
- TPR and reenactment. Books with action verbs for teaching comprehension for TPR, and books with actionable scenes for reenactment.
- Visualizing. Books teaching vocabulary with illustrations, such as semantically organized picture dictionaries, and concept books.

The organization of this book corresponds with these four criteria: CLT principles, topic, language difficulty, and CLT strategies as described above.

CONTENT

Chapter 1 introduces the first step in selecting books with tellability, that is, books that are compatible with the basic principles of a balanced CLT program. Picture books must have features compatible with oral and written comprehension, as well as expression, language-focused learning, and fluency. As with all the chapters, the book examples in this chapter revolve around a theme. The theme for the book examples in this chapter is butterflies.

Chapter 2 considers the interplay of content and language in selecting books that will be a bridge between beginner ELP and academic English. Basically, books with the right topics for beginners are about concrete concepts and themes, which are useful for vocabulary as well as other aspects of language learning. In addition, they must be interesting to school-aged ELLs. The books cited in this chapter are content oriented and include animals and topics related to science, social studies, mathematics, and language arts.

Chapter 3 addresses beginner language difficulty. Beginner ELLs' perception of their ability to successfully express themselves in English changes when books match their ELP. Therefore, it is important for their success to divide the broad level of beginner ELP into stages along the beginner ELP level continuum. The four stages described in this chapter were determined by examining the interplay between the amount of language in the book and its complexity. The first stage includes the easiest books. They are short and have simple language, while books for the fourth stage are longer and more complex. In between are books with different interplays of amount and complexity. The theme of the sample books in Chapter 3 is plants.

Chapter 4 describes informal assessments used to find the right books for each ELL stage of beginning. Within the context of teaching with a picture book, the assessments address questions about the ELL's English oral and written abilities. The information collected with these assessments allows the teacher to select the right book for ELLs. Continuous assessment during book-based teaching is essential, because beginners differ widely in the pace at which they develop oral and written skills. Chapter 4 book examples are about transportation.

Chapter 5 describes the last essential step in the process of finding books with *tellability*, matching books to CLT strategies. The twelve CLT strategies mentioned earlier in the preface are each linked to a type of book format. The strategies covered have a balance of skills and address communicative competencies. The theme of books cited is tiny animals.

The appendix includes three units with four lesson plans each and a book list for every lesson plan. These book lists are associated with the units' themes: cats, food, and people. Each lesson presents an anchor book, the focus CLT strategy, and other CLT strategies to focus on comprehension, expression, language-focused learning, and fluency. The first unit on cats includes the strategies TPR, retelling, guessing games, and reader's theater. The second on food includes realia, LEA, compare and contrast, and chanting and singing. The third is about people and uses visualizing, model-based writing, graphics, and recitation.

Annotated book lists in the appendix and at the end of each chapter address eight themes and the 12 CLT strategies. Additional books on other topics are listed on the book's web page at http://www.corwin.com/picturebooks4ells. I hope these lists reduce the time you spend searching for the right books for your ELL students.

Finally, although analyzing the particular features of picture books helps with lesson planning, remember that by dissecting the content, graphics, and nuances in the pages of a book, no one ever gathered in the beauty of experiencing it with another person.

NOTES

1. I prefer using the phrase *communicative language teaching* (CLT) to others, such as *teaching English to speakers of other languages* (TESOL), because of my focus on teaching communicative competency.

2. My use of *tellability* also derives from storytelling and narrative analysis, where it refers to features that make a story worth telling independent from its text. It considers the narrator's ability to raise the interest of, interact with, and adapt to a given audience (Herman, Jahn, & Ryan, 2005; Labov, 1972). My tellability focus is on the use of multiple genre picture books as prompts for teacher instructional interactions with beginning ELLs.

Acknowledgments

Corwin gratefully acknowledges the contributions of the following reviewers:

Quan Cao
Executive Director
Alliance for Multilingual
Multicultural Education
(AMME)
Boca Raton, FL

Blanca L. Campillo
Professional Development
Specialist
Area 9
Chicago Public Schools
Chicago, IL

Michelle DaCosta
Elementary Curriculum
Resource Specialist
Bilingual Education Department
Framingham Public Schools
Framingham, MA

Jacqueline Hickey
Elementary ESL Facilitator
Westerville City School District
Westerville, OH

Mari Rasmussen
Board Member
National Council of State Title III
Directors
Washington, DC
National Clearinghouse for
English Language Acquisition
George Washington University
Washington, DC

Esmer Wear
Elementary ESL/Immigrant
Program Coordinator
Plano Independent
School District
Plano, TX

Lana Whitaker
Teacher and Reading Specialist
Reading First Coach K–3
Chandler's Elementary School
Russellville, KY

Diane Zimmerman
Superintendent
Old Adobe Union School District
Petaluma, CA

About the Author

Ana Lado began her teaching career as a bilingual kindergarten and preschool literacy teacher in Washington, D.C. Teaching Spanish and English to younger students is still one of her favorite activities. She is a frequent presenter at local schools, regional conferences, and international conventions.

In 1992, she obtained her PhD in applied linguistics from Georgetown University in Washington, D.C. She is currently a professor in the School of Education and Human Services at Marymount University in Arlington, Virginia. She coordinates the Master of Education program in Teaching English as a Second Language (TESOL) and advises graduate students in the Master of Education program in Professional Studies. Her favorite courses involve TESOL and reading. She also enjoys courses exploring educational issues related to bilingualism, multicultural language arts, and creativity.

In addition to teaching at Marymount, she conducts academic training and material development for LADO International College. This private school—founded by her father, Robert Lado, in the 1970s—provides intensive, accelerated, English classes for speakers of other languages. Her current materials development project is a revision of the Lado English Series texts. Her current academic training work is with Lado's certificate program in Teaching English as a Foreign Language (TEFL).

Using Picture Books With English Language Learners

I love everything about children's picture books. They appeal to me visually, linguistically, and socially. I find the complex synergy between image and word fascinating (Galda, Sullivan, & Sipe, 2007; Nikolajeva & Scott, 2006). By far, picture books are my favorite resource for teaching language and literacy. I like the classics, and I also enjoy postmodern picture books that engage readers by blurring the traditional boundaries between written and spoken communication with interactive questions and other innovative formats (Galda et al., 2008; Nolde, 2008).

Picture books are a flexible resource. They are well suited to teaching beginner English language learners (ELLs) in grades K–12. Although a smaller percentage of picture books have topics of interest to high school beginners, some books can be found to match their needs. In fact, picture books can be found to meet the needs of ELLs from a diversity of backgrounds and in different levels of English language proficiency (ELP).[1]

BOOKS FOR ELLS

ELP is a developmental continuum. For practical programmatic reasons, it is divided into identifiable levels of ability (Boyd-Batstone, 2006; Richard-Amato & Snow, 2005; Rothenberg & Fisher 2007).[2] For communicative language teaching (CLT) to be effective, instruction must use materials and strategies within ELLs' ELP range. Although programs differ, the beginner level of ELP is composed of ELLs with common novice-level characteristics. The materials and strategies used with them should reflect their instructional range and unique linguistic needs.

One of the most basic principles of second-language teaching is based on the fact that the English spoken between native speakers is too difficult for beginner ELLs. It is not within their range and does not meet their linguistic processing requirements. When listening to native speakers, beginners are overwhelmed just trying to grasp the basic units. Breakdowns in communication are the norm. In order to avoid breakdowns, teachers of ELLs modify their speech. They simplify it. For example, when talking about or reading a book, the teacher adjusts the amount of simplification depending on the difference between the English in the book and that known by the ELL.

The most common mediation strategies enhance ELLs' comprehension and access to English. These strategies are multidimensional (August & Shanahan, 2006; Hadaway, Vardell, & Young, 2006; Tabors, 1997; Uso-Juan & Martinez-Flor, 2006). For example, teachers scaffold comprehension with verbal and nonverbal scaffolds, such as pictures, gestures, objects, and native language. They provide models of English with controlled language, such as short, simplified, patterned, repeated, and highlighted samples. Teachers focus on providing beginner ELLs with comprehensible and accessible English.

In CLT, the use of a controlled language sample is necessary and usual. It focuses attention on a manageable amount of language, and, thus, reduces miscommunication and accelerates language learning (Chaudron, 1988; Lado, 1988; Long, 1985; Rost, 2006). Carefully selected picture books offer one way to provide a controlled language sample. Their inherent scaffolds provide models for written and oral beginner responses. These books are relevant, accessible, and authentic, and they provide opportunities for deep language processing. They pave the way for further communicative tasks and foment language development.

The current practice in book selection for ELLs combines the two fields of reading and teaching English to speakers of other languages (TESOL). In reading, a book's difficulty level is generally determined using a readability formula. These formulas incorporate relevant linguistic variables, such as syntactic complexity and vocabulary complexity. In addition, Harris and Hodges (2005)[3] emphasize the importance of other variables associated with reader characteristics, such as age, and the instructional context, such as grade-level connections of the reading material.

Each of these—the linguistic, student, and contextual variables—is distinct and considered in book selection in TESOL. In selecting books for TESOL, it is imperative to consider linguistic variables associated with different ELP levels. Books with simpler syntax and vocabulary are easier. Reader characteristics are an important variable in TESOL. In addition to age, book selection often considers student backgrounds, education, and culture. Additionally, TESOL instructional contexts are distinct from contexts for reading, because oral language is taught along with literacy.

Unfortunately, ELP-level designations of trade books are broadly construed. Designations for books found on lists will over- or underestimate the ability of ELLs. The beginner ELP level, in particular, incorporates a wide range of books, many of which are beyond the abilities of ELLs at the earliest stages. Teachers have several options in adjusting to this situation (Allen, 1994; Chamot & O'Malley, 1994; Hadaway, 2009; Rost, 2006; Smallwood, 2002). Unlike reading teachers who mediate with English speakers using oral language elaborations to fill in meaning, teachers of second-language learners simplify their language. Simplification combines linguistic scaffolds, such as easier English, with nonlinguistic scaffolds, such as pictures. Its purpose is twofold. It facilitates ELLs' participation by bridging the gap between their English abilities and the difficult English required in a given situation. It also promotes language learning.

SIMPLIFICATION

Teacher simplification between text and students is complex. A typical example of planned simplification is when a teacher divides a book into sections and also teaches the oral and written responses separately. Teachers plan the language they use according to the ELLs' abilities. When that preplanning does not go far enough, teachers spontaneously implement more adjustments. Their linguistic adjustments are flexible and highly dependent on student responses. Simplification, a teacher's adjustment to the linguistic abilities of ELLs, is an essential CLT tool. It is manifested in a variety of strategies, such as scaffolding,[4] accommodating, frontloading, and contextualizing.[5]

These simplifications are focused on helping ELLs grasp the layers of interrelated linguistic forms associated with meaningful communication. "*Scaffolding* [emphasis added] refers to providing contextual supports for meaning through the use of simplified language, teacher modeling, visuals and graphics, cooperative learning and hands-on learning" (Ovando, Collier, & Combs, 2003, p. 345). *Accommodations* refer to practices intended to increase access to grade-level content. *Frontloading* is providing essential information and key vocabulary before a lesson begins (Calderon, 2007). *Contextualizing* refers to providing explanations and meaning through situational information. The use of context helps ELLs grasp the meaning of new language by using information from the circumstances in which something happens as well as from the other words or phrases surrounding the new language.

The amount and type of simplification are directly proportional to the difference between the language of a book and that known by the student (Gottlieb, Cranely, & Oliver, 2007; Opitz & Guccione, 2009; Pantaleo, 2004). In the case of beginners, teachers incrementally expose them to new units and patterns of phonemes, morphemes, sentence units, discourse structures, and other aspects of communicative competency (Davison & Kantor, 1982; Rothenberg & Fisher, 2007). To be successful, beginners must dedicate attention and effort, and teachers must simplify across many levels of English communication.

TELLABILITY

My approach to simplification is to lessen the gap between student's ELP and the books the student uses. I select books with features that closely match beginner abilities while promoting language learning. These features provide teachers with built-in simplifications, thus reducing the amount of teacher adjustments and giving ELLs more access to the English of the text. Every picture book has a combination of embedded verbal, visual, and experiential scaffolds.

The most interesting features of picture books for our purpose are those that combine to make a picture book close to the English ability of an ELL. These include the typical types of simplifications used in CLT, including simpler forms of English, but also certain text patterns, illustrations, themes, and formats.

An examination of these features allows us to rank picture books within the beginner ELP level. Beginner-level picture books can be divided into four groups of language difficulty. For ELLs in the first stage of the beginner level, we want to use books with the simplest language with many embedded simplifications. For example, Stage 1 books meet the earliest beginner's need for pictures that make the meaning of the text clear. In contrast, at the other extreme are books for beginners in the last stage of the beginner level. Such Stage 4 books include more language and have fewer embedded simplifications, because at this stage the ELLs are able to process more English.

As stated in the preface, I describe picture books for teaching beginner ELLs with the terms *tellable* and *tellability*. I use these terms as a reminder to focus attention on oral language learning and creating synchronicities between many different aspects of communication. Books with tellability are accessible to beginners and compatible with beginner ELL needs. They provide the following:

1. comprehensible input, meaningful expressive output, language-focused learning, and fluency building;

2. thematic vocabulary;

3. incremental exposure to English within the beginner ELP level; and

4. models for responding to books.

As the following Dr. Seuss Day vignette demonstrates, using a book with tellability makes a striking difference in student success. It also reduces a teacher's need to develop materials for simplification.

DR. SEUSS DAY VIGNETTE

On Dr. Seuss's birthday I was tapped to read books in Spanish with a small group of beginning ELLs. The idea was to help them fully enjoy the event. As soon as I finished sharing the first Dr. Seuss Day book in Spanish, it became obvious they wanted to participate in English when a girl picked up a picture dictionary. She methodically turned the pages until she reached the illustration of a giraffe. Deliberately tracking each letter of the labeled picture, she said, "giraffe" then "like." She then continued paging through the dictionary and proudly pointed to a picture and said, "zebra." Her interest in the picture dictionary made me shift gears in several ways.

First, I taught them noun phrases in groups of four phrases. I divided a paper into a two-by-two grid (four sections) and wrote one noun phrase in each section, for example, *big zebra, little zebra, big giraffe,* and *little giraffe.* They practiced reading the grid, made a picture card for each phrase, and matched cards to it. Gradually they were weaned off the grid and could read the cards randomly and substitute them into a question/answer routine: "Which animal do you like?" "I like the ___."

Second, I took a book from the shelf with tellability features. This book, *From Head to Toe* (Carle, 2003), has simple repetitive language and clear pictures. It presents 12 animals, 12 body parts, and 12 actions in patterned sentences. The students learned these with the aid of pictures and gestures. They substituted words, "I am a(n) (animal name)" and "I (action taken) my (body part)." In playful give and take, we expanded to responding with negatives and plurals.

Third, they memorized the repetitive lines, the animals each asking whether the boy can do take the given action, and the boy always answering that he can.

Finally, as an expansion activity, they made a sequel[6] using a fold-a-book[7] technique resulting in a tiny eight-page book. *From Head to Toe* was the right book from which to explore, discover, stretch, and develop their English abilities.

This book is probably on every book list for beginner ELLs. It has a low readability level, is easy to understand, has a culturally neutral topic, and is produced by an award-winning popular author–illustrator. It supports the basics of CLT by having pictures as scaffolds for comprehension, oral style sentences for expression, patterns for language-focused learning, and repetition for building fluency. However, I also selected it because its topic matched the age of the students, their specific stage of beginner ELP, and the CLT strategies that I use with beginners. I like unison oral repetition, choral reading, substituting words in patterned sentences, and gesturing.

Using *From Head to Toe,* a book with so many features that matched the ELLs' needs, was such a contrast to the picture dictionary on many levels, all of which are reasons to categorize it as being tellable. The following section provides examples of books with tellable features. The theme of the examples is butterflies.

BOOKS WITH TELLABLE FEATURES FOR A UNIT ON BUTTERFLIES

Picture books about butterflies represent an enormous variety of styles and links among textual, visual, and format features. Butterfly-themed books provide opportunities for recursive learning of vocabulary and incremental pacing of instruction. The idea is to guide beginners through the early language acquisition process with the simplest books until they are ready for more challenging content. For example, some of the books introduce science concepts, such as the life cycle, and help ELLs develop comprehension.

The samples listed here begin with the simplest books in order to focus on teaching basic comprehension, the first strand of a balanced CLT program. They are followed by other types of books usable for developing expression, the second strand. Different genres of picture books are included to provide ELLs with opportunities to practice oral and written expression, such as first person narratives for dramatic activities and patterned formats for reading aloud. ELLs also need opportunities for language-focused learning. An example of a book addressing this strand is one with maps about butterfly migration. ELLs can focus on learning the content language used with mapping. Finally, a balanced CLT program includes a fourth strand, building fluency. Fluency is promoted in several ways, such as the recurrence of thematic vocabulary, the use of books with repetitious text, and the use of short books that can be reread.

First Strand: Focus on Comprehension

Beginners need to comprehend the language sample in order to learn it. A balanced language-teaching program begins with teaching comprehension of essential words presented in oral and written forms. The first teaching strategies empower ELLs to demonstrate receptive comprehension skills independently from expression skills. ELLs learn vocabulary about concrete concepts by hearing, seeing, and imitating words as separate units. They learn to identify words within a phrase or sentence. The teaching strategies should engage them in activities that demand comprehension and forming associations between a word's oral and written forms.

Strategies for teaching comprehension empower ELLs to demonstrate receptive comprehension skills independently of the ELLs' ability to express themselves in English. The earliest beginners do not have to be overwhelmed with both receptive and expressive skills at once. They can focus on demonstrating ability to understand and leave learning the expression for later. Thus, many beginner comprehension strategies use visuals, objects, gestures, and native language. These allow the ELL to show comprehension by nonlinguistic or non-English means while, at the same time, ensuring the student is connecting the concept with the correct English word or label. For example, ELLs demonstrate that they understand the word by pointing to a visual, selecting an object, physically moving in response to a directive, or saying the English word in their native language. Several picture books about butterflies lend themselves to CLT strategies focusing on beginner comprehension. These strategies include visualizing, realia, total physical response (TPR), and reenactment.

Using visuals is one of the most common strategies used with beginner ELLs. Its use includes everything from photographs to picture cards, to student drawings, to text illustrations. The term *visualizing* in education can refer to a number of different activities. Here it refers to a language-teaching strategy based on visuals. The book *Born to Be a Butterfly* (Wallace, 2000) lends itself to visualizing, because each sentence in its text is accompanied by a photograph.

Using objects is another popular language teaching strategy. Concrete manipulatives help ELLs grasp the distinctive words and retain them in memory. The term *realia* is used for strategies using instructional objects, artifacts, and models. Realia help beginners demonstrate comprehension of nouns and actions with them, such as following directives, for example, to touch, select, give, bring, or put away a particular object. Examples of books that lend themselves to realia are *Caterpillar Spring, Butterfly Summer* (Hood, 2003) and *The Very Hungry Caterpillar Pop-Up Book* (Carle, 2009). *Caterpillar Spring, Butterfly Summer* contains a slinky caterpillar on every page. *The Very Hungry Caterpillar Pop-Up Book* has embedded paper objects that lift from the page, for example, a half-cylinder tree trunk.

Using gestures is a standard strategy in teaching ELLs comprehension of verbs. Two well-known language teaching strategies using gestures are total physical response and reenactment. *Total physical response* is so popular with beginners that teachers often refer to it as TPR. In TPR, teachers act out the meaning of a verb, and students learn through imitation. It is a useful strategy to use with texts with active verbs. Teachers can preview the verbs with TPR. Once each is understood, the ELLs can proceed to learning the rest of the text. *Reenactment* is simply the strategy in which students act out the scenes of a story. It is useful because ELLs can demonstrate their understanding of a sequence of scenes. Both TPR and reenactment are easy to use with *Caterpillar Spring, Butterfly Summer*, mentioned above. A tiny board book with a short poem, *One Little Butterfly* (Lewison, 2000) also lends itself to TPR and reenactment, because its poetic text contains ten verbs.

Second Strand: Focus on Expression

A balanced CLT program includes teaching expression. It is essential that ELLs be provided opportunities to learn to express their needs, make their desires known, exchange information, and give opinions. Several picture books about butterflies lend themselves to CLT strategies focusing on expression: retelling, the language experience approach (LEA), and model-based writing.

Retelling is one of the easiest ways to build expressive skills. Picture books lend themselves to it, because students use the pictures as a scaffold. In addition, stories with sequential plots and books about a sequential concept lend themselves to retelling. The fascinating process of metamorphosis is a natural match for retelling. Some book examples for retelling are *Butterfly* (Canizares, 1998), *From Caterpillar to Butterfly* (Legg, 1998), and *Butterflies and Caterpillars* (Ganeri, 2007).

The *Language Experience Approach* teaches written language by using students' oral language to create reading material. In its most frequently used form, the students dictate their experiences, and the teacher writes their words on a LEA chart. For beginner ELLs, this strategy requires modification, because they need models to express themselves about the experience. Books about projects, memorable experiences, directions, or procedures provide the ELLs with models for oral and written expression. They can use the text or pictures to guide them during the experience and later in the dictation. The end pages of *Monarch Butterfly* (Gibbons, 1991) and *Butterfly House* (Bunting, 1999) contain directions for making a butterfly habitat. Ross's *Crafts for Kids Who Are Learning About Insects* (2008) contains procedures for making six butterfly crafts.

Model-based writing is used with beginner ELLs because they are still developing written expression and benefit from controlled activities that explicitly focus on writing. In model-based writing, ELLs become familiar with a text, copy it as a starting point, use it as a template upon which to construct their own ideas, and go from there to developing writing that is intelligible, coherent, and cohesive. They gradually build the ability to use picture book texts as springboards for personally generated and creative written pieces. Two books that contain models of simple writing skills, such as appropriate pronoun usage, are *Waiting for Wings* (Ehlert, 2001) and *Born to Be a Butterfly* (Wallace, 2000).

Third Strand: Language-Focused Learning

Spending a reasonable amount of time in language-focused learning activities is of enormous benefit to school-aged ELLs (Calderon, 2004; Hadaway, Vardell, & Young, 2006; Nation, 2001; Uribe & Nathenson-Mejía, 2008). An efficient CLT program provides ELLs with explicit language-focused learning activities. ELLs benefit from opportunities to consciously practice the subsystems of English they are learning, because language-focused learning "involves deliberate attention to language features both in the context of meaning-focused input and meaning-focused output, and in decontextualised learning and teaching" (Nation, 2001, p. 1).

Language-focused learning strategies used with ELLs build upon the types of strategies used in teaching language arts to native speakers. They provide additional steps to scaffolding comprehension, adding practice opportunities, and involving ELLs in recognizing English patterns for imitation, substitution, analysis, manipulation, and utilization (Nation, 2001). With picture books, I use three types of language-focused learning strategies: compare and contrast, graphics, and guessing games.

Compare and contrast can be applied in different ways depending on the features of picture books. First, bilingual texts lend themselves to teaching English through having ELLs contrast, compare, and reflect on similarities and differences between their native language and English. An example of a book with this feature is the earlier mentioned *Butterfly*. There is a bilingual version, *Butterfly/Mariposa* (English/Spanish) (Canizares, 2003). Second, texts of different genres lend themselves to learning about different discourse styles. Teachers can use a single book that contains multiple genres or several books of different types. *Monarch Butterfly* (Gibbons, 1991) is an example of a multigenre book. The running narrative explains the life cycle, while the end pages are directions for raising monarch butterflies. The books *Butterfly* (Ling, 2007) and *I'm a Caterpillar* (Marzollo, 1997) represent different genres. Students can use these two books to compare and contrast nonfiction discourse and its use of photographs with fictional stories told by the insect with illustrations. Third, some books present content in ways that lend themselves to comparing and contrasting. A book with parallel descriptions of different types of butterflies is *Butterflies and Caterpillars* (Berger, 2008).

Graphics and graphic organizers are a staple in teaching students to represent information and relationships among concepts. Common examples used to teach ELLs vocabulary and text structure are story maps, story webs, concept maps, and semantic maps (Echevarria, Vogt, & Short, 2008). Picture books with graphics provide an ideal venue for learning to interpret graphic information and transfer between verbal and visual representations. *Are You a Butterfly?* (Allen, 2000a) is an example of a simple way in which graphic information is represented in picture books. This book uses a special font as an aid to meaning; for example, the word *grow* appears in letters that increase in size: **grOW**. *Monarch and Milkweed* (Frost, 2008) is an example of a text with a graphic organizer, a time line. It, along with *Hurry and the Monarch* (Flatharta, 2009), contains maps explaining butterfly migration. *A Monarch Butterfly's Life* (Himmelman, 2000) includes two types of text. Each lends itself to a different type of graphic organizer: the sequential narrative to a story map and the glossary to a semantic map.

Books with *guessing game* formats create opportunities to learn inquiry formulas and patterns. ELLs benefit from practicing routines with questions and answers using familiar, as well as new, information. When they are involved in inquiry about new information, this is referred to as an *information gap* task. Books mentioned earlier with interactive questions in the text are *Butterflies and Caterpillars* and *Are You a Butterfly?*

Fourth Strand: Fluency Development

Fluency is the fourth strand of a balanced CLT program. ELLs must be given time and sustained opportunities to practice language in order to increase their accuracy, intonation, and pace. Rereading and rewriting tasks improve fluency. Three types of sparse-text books lend themselves to repetition by using oral chanting, recitation, and reader's theater.

Chanting is an oral strategy requiring students to repeat phrases in unison. Oral-style picture books are compatible with chanting. Canizares's *Butterfly*, mentioned earlier, is easily reread and chanted.

Some of the books in this theme are short and poetic. These lend themselves to *recitation* and are used in a poetry reading or recital. *A New Butterfly: My First Look at Metamorphosis* (Hickman & Collins, 1997a) consists of repetitive cumulative verses, and *Caterpillar Spring, Butterfly Summer* (Hood, 2003) contains catchy rhymes.

Picture books with first person dialogue are useful for *reader's theater*. Reader's theater involves oral reading of a script or text with a focus on the oral expression rather than props. *I'm a Caterpillar* (Marzollo, 1997) is relatively easy, with about 150 words of running text. *Hurry and the Monarch* (Flatharta, 2009), mentioned earlier, is longer but contains humorous lines that older students enjoy.

BUTTERFLY BOOKS FOR ELLS

The books in Box 1.1 are listed in three groups. The first is a group of the easiest and shortest to use with the earliest beginner ELL. This is followed by a middle category for expanding vocabulary and opportunities for interactions. The third group includes longer books that provide opportunities for deep processing of the thematic vocabulary but include much more variety and opportunities to learn English. The third group would have been overwhelming for true beginner ELLs. However, after exposure to the language and activities associated with the earlier books, they are better prepared for accessing and learning from these books.

Box 1.1   Butterfly Books in Alphabetical Order and Grouped by Difficulty

1. *Born to Be a Butterfly* (Wallace, 2000)*
   Butterfly (Canizares, 1998)*
   Butterfly/Mariposa (Canizares, 2003)*
   I'm a Caterpillar (Marzollo, 1997)
   One Little Butterfly (Lewison, 2000)

2. *Are You a Butterfly?* (Allen, 2000a)
   Butterflies and Caterpillars (Ganeri, 2007)
   Butterfly (Ling, 2007)*
   Caterpillar Spring, Butterfly Summer (Hood, 2003)
   From Caterpillar to Butterfly (Legg, 1998)*
   A Monarch Butterfly's Life (Himmelman, 2000)*
   A New Butterfly: My First Look at Metamorphosis (Hickman & Collins, 1997a)*
   Waiting for Wings (Ehlert, 2001)

3. *Butterflies and Caterpillars* (Berger, 2008)*
   Butterfly House (Bunting, 1999)*
   Hurry and the Monarch (Flatharta, 2009)*
   Monarch and Milkweed (Frost, 2008)*
   Monarch Butterfly (Gibbons, 1991)*
   The Very Hungry Caterpillar Pop-Up Book (Carle, 2009)

---

*Appropriate for ELLs in upper grades.

CONCLUSION

Teachers and ELLs benefit when books match their second-language learning needs. Books must be within beginners' capacity to comprehend, express, practice, and engage in language-focused learning and fluency development.

Books that support CLT are important because they create synchron-icities between students, text, visuals, and instructional experiences. The process of finding these books involves more than what is usually contained in formulas focused on reading. The best books are not just readable; they are tellable, as they meet the needs of beginner ELLs.

One of the specific ways to select books for their tellability is to focus on a theme. Themes maximize opportunities for language and content learning. Along with themes, select books according to whether the content is of appropriate difficulty, usability, and interest. These areas are discussed in Chapter 2.

TELLABILITY IN PRACTICE: USING CLT CRITERIA

Select one of the books from the list in Box 1.1. Evaluate it according to the concepts discussed in the chapter. Next, select a book from your classroom, library, or bookstore, and analyze it in the same way.

1.1. What book features are associated with CLT lesson planning for comprehension, expression, language-focused learning, or fluency development?

1.2. Which of these features does the book have?

NOTES

1. State departments of education divide ELP into levels. The TESOL organization divides ELP into five: starting, emerging, developing, expanding, and bridging (Gottlieb, 2006). Beginner-level ELP corresponds to what is often referred to as a *starting* and *emerging* level.

2. I also find the description of beginner second-language learners in the ACTFL proficiency levels useful; see http://www.actfl.org.

3. Formulas for estimating a text's difficulty vary (Bauman, 1995; Fountas & Pinnell, 2005; Fry, 2002; Gunning, 1999; Harris & Hodges, 1995). Every readability formula measures vocabulary and sentence variables. Leveled book formulas also include variables associated with initial literacy, such as the match of illustrations to text.

4. Scaffolding is the subject of a book by Gibbons (2002).

5. Frontloading is providing essential information and key vocabulary before a lesson begins.

6. Deeb and Jakar (2009) have a good description of how to do this type of "book after a book" project with ELLs.

7. For directions on making a fold-a-book, see Yopp and Yopp (2006). Also, online directions can be found at http://www.readwritethink.org/parent-after school-resources/games-tools/video/stapleless-book-a-30190.html and http://www.bookmakingwithkids.com/wp-content/uploads/2008/11/single-sheet-books.pdf

Selecting Books With the Right Content Difficulty

Sometimes when browsing a bookshelf, it is possible to find just the right book by chance. Its language and content are within the abilities of the group of beginner English language learners (ELLs) I am teaching. Its topic is suited to their abilities and pertinent to a topic covered in their grade. Additionally, the content is presented in ways that lend themselves to teaching ELLs. For example, the book contains a challenging amount of content but not enough to overwhelm or interfere with the ELLs' language acquisition. However, most of the time finding a picture book with the right content for school-age beginners is a time-consuming process. It requires evaluating whether the content itself and the manner in which it is presented is within the instructional range of the ELLs. Doing this requires knowing who the students are, what they know, and what they can do.

Examining the content of a picture book is a critical step to determining a book's tellability for several reasons. Beginner ELLs must be able to understand the content to be able to learn the language. At the same time, they must experience language in context and not as a subject. It is the medium for further developing knowledge about the world in general and about school subjects in particular (Hadaway & Mundy, 1999; National Reading Panel, 2000; Wong-Fillmore & Snow, 2000). Teachers must carefully vet the content in picture books to select those with the right type and amount of content to maximize language learning. This can be done by asking the following basic questions:

1. How cognitively *difficult* is the content?

2. How *useful* is it?

3. How *interesting* is it?

1. HOW COGNITIVELY DIFFICULT IS THE CONTENT?

Content difficulty in picture books is by its very nature multidimensional. Difficulty is the result of several related factors—the content itself, the way this is presented, and the students involved. Often the content of picture books is basic and simplistic. This is because many authors assume a young audience. For beginning ELLs this type of book poses no barriers. However, a good number of picture books contain complex and culturally laden content that poses barriers to comprehension. Traditionally, picture books presented content in a straightforward style of text with complementary illustrations. Today's postmodern picture books have a wide range of presentation styles. Many of these contain complex concepts and relationships between text and illustrations. They blur traditional boundaries of written text, oral language, genres, illustrations, and electronic media. Finally, the concept of content difficulty depends on the knowledge and abilities of the readers. For example, beginner ELLs who are older will find a particular picture book about a general topic easy, while those who are younger would find it a challenge.

A good place to begin examining the content challenges of picture books is the work of Cummins (1981, 1991), who examined the difficulty of schoolbooks for ELLs. He popularized a way of describing content difficulty in conjunction with linguistic and context factors. In his view, difficulty is the result of the interplay of two intersecting continua, language and cognitive demands. The language continuum ranges from one extreme of easy language used in contextually embedded ways to the opposite extreme of much more difficult academic language used in a context-reduced manner. The content continuum ranges from cognitively undemanding information that requires little processing to cognitively demanding information. This intersection of language and content continua results in four quadrants (see Box 2.1).

Quadrant A represents situations that have context-embedded clues to language meaning *and* have undemanding content. The types of books that would fall within this quadrant allow ELLs opportunities for deep processing of meaningful, accessible, and easy language. They contain multiple sources of support for comprehension, such as transparent illustrations to make text meaning clear, and sequential order for easy processing. They contain manageable amounts of new words presented in formats that lend themselves to language development activities, such as word recognition, parsing, repetition, and sentence embedding. One example would be a picture book about counting with an interactive oral-style text. It would fall into Quadrant A because the undemanding topic is presented with linguistic, visual, and social supports.

Books in Quadrant D represent the opposite situation of A. The texts have few clues to aid understanding and have cognitively demanding content. An example of a book falling into this quadrant is an academic text used for intense study, such as a summary of concepts or an anthology of poems. It

---

Box 2.1   Range of Contextual Support and Degree of Cognitive Demands in Picture Books

Cognitively Undemanding (easy) A and C

A. **Contextually Embedded Language (clues) and Cognitively Undemanding Content (easy)**	C. **Context-Reduced language (few clues) and Cognitively Undemanding Content (easy)**
Picture books with easy, accessible language and content. The format lends itself to hands-on and unison activities with linguistic, visual, and social supports.	Picture books with less accessible language yet an easy topic. The text might have a dense style and lack clarifying illustrations. Yet the topic is concrete and familiar.
B. **Contextually Embedded Language (clues) and Cognitively Demanding Content (difficult)** Picture books with accessible language and demanding content. The text might have an oral style, transparent illustration, and patterned language, but the content is unfamiliar, academic, or abstract.	D. **Context-Reduced Language (few clues) and Cognitively Demanding Content (difficult)** Picture books containing demanding content that use language presented without contextual clues. The book's format might require topic-specific vocabulary and skills and contain few linguistic, visual, and social supports.

Cognitively Demanding (difficult) B and D

Source: Adapted from Cummins (1981, p. 12). Reprinted with permission.

would fall into Quadrant D because it requires topic-specific vocabulary and skills and it contains few linguistic, visual, and social supports.

In between these two extremes are Quadrants B and C. Quadrant B represents situations with context-embedded language yet difficult content. For example, just as in Quadrant A, the meaning of text is supported through patterned language, clear illustrations that closely match the text, and an oral style lending itself to experiential activities. However, unlike the content in books found in Quadrant A, the content would be unfamiliar, abstract, or academic. A picture book example would be a book about imperial units of measurement with illustrations transparently illustrating these units. It would fall into Quadrant B because the content would be unfamiliar to ELLs who have either a metric system background or limited formal schooling.

Quadrant C would contain books with the opposite balance of Quadrant B: The language is dense and less accessible because it lacks contextual cues, such as clarifying illustrations. At the same time, the content is undemanding. An example would be a book with tongue-twisting rhymes about a palpable, concrete, and familiar concept, such as a sophisticated set of riddles about counting from 1 to 10.

Cummins's framework is a useful way to analyze the content difficulty of picture books. It introduces the critical factors of the demands of the content, given the language needs of second language learners.

There is an enormous body of research on the influence of learner characteristics on language learning (August & Shanahan, 2006; Coggins, Kravin, Coats, & Carroll, 2007; Dutro & Moran, 2005; Echevarria & Graves, 2007; Genesee, Lindholm-Leary, Saunders, & Christian, 2005; Nisbet & Tindall, 2006). Simply put, whether a book is cognitively demanding depends on the students' ages, English language proficiency (ELP) levels, educational backgrounds, cultures, and other characteristics. Those student characteristics central to selecting picture books for beginner ELLs will be explored here. These are their ages, literacy levels, educational backgrounds, and cultures.

Age

We know that cognitive abilities are related to age (Long, 1990b). Thus, whether a picture book is of appropriate difficulty for beginner ELLs has a lot to do with their ages. Age is a determining factor in their ability to understand the content of a book, either because they are developmentally ready to understand it or because they have already learned the subject or skill. Juxtaposing examples of picture books with different content demands can illustrate ways the ages of ELLs are relevant to their ability to access, grasp, and learn. Four examples suffice: Crews's *Ten Black Dots* (1995b) and *Bicycle Race* (1985), Giganti and Crews's *How Many Birds Flew Away? A Counting Book With a Difference* (2005), and Nolan's *How Much, How Many, How Far, How Heavy, How Long, How Tall Is 1000?* (1995).

Ten Black Dots, a book about counting from 1 to 10, is the easiest among these. Each page illustrates a quantity with dots. The dots are incorporated into illustrations of objects. The number and numeral are introduced with brief and easy-to-memorize rhyming lines. The end pages review the concepts with pyramid diagrams in ascending order from 1 to 5 and 6 to 10. This book's format lends itself to teaching with unison chanting and with matching and sorting tasks.

Bicycle Race poses increased challenges because it requires students to do more than repeat a rhyme in unison and match text. There is a story line to follow. The numbers 1 through 12 identify the number of riders, and a numeral is used as an identification label for each rider. The riders change positions in each leg of the race. Teachers would not expect ELLs to memorize the lists of riders, but they can chant the cheers of the audience in unison and reenact each scene. I would have ELLs shuffle themselves into each arrangement of riders and, thus, use inquiry-based interactions among themselves. The text contains questions; this is a typical strategy for teaching mathematic content (Coggins et al., 2009). In sum, this book requires ELLs to use language with more independence than the previous book does.

How Many Birds Flew Away? A Counting Book With a Difference is organized in a way that is typical of Giganti; the illustrations are double-page spreads featuring a set of rhythmic, repetitious questions instructing the reader to calculate the quantities of one type of item as compared to another. For example, one spread has questions about the number of pencils and pens in the illustration and the differences between these two quantities. This book requires readers to know basic addition and subtraction as they solve the visual puzzles.

How Much, How Many, How Far, How Heavy, How Long, How Tall Is 1000? contains even more mathematics and language content and assumes an older reader. Its text is organized around questions about the number 1,000. For example, readers are asked to differentiate between 1,000 stacked sheets of paper and 1,000 pages blown across a large area, or between 1,000 people sitting in an arena and 1,000 people waiting in line outside.

These examples illustrate the importance of considering ELLs' ages when examining the level of difficulty posed by a picture book's content. They also demonstrate the effects of education and literacy. ELLs are not just learning English; they are learning it in a school context. Therefore, the academic skills they bring to the task will influence whether they find it difficult or easy.

Education and Literacy

Education and literacy in one's first language teaches students to make connections between oral and written language. Educational experiences facilitate ELLs' ability to interpret content presented in various forms, written language, visually, and through instructional activities. This applies to the content presented in picture books.

Literate ELLs are able to apply general literacy concepts to approaching, deciphering, and interpreting written English text (Hickman, Pollard-Durodola, & Vaughn, 2004). Among literate ELLs, those who are literate in the Roman alphabet have an advantage. They begin at a place that is further along the ELP continuum because they do not have to learn the written forms at the same time as they learn the content. They already know the relationships between different fonts and scripts. Not only do they start at a different point, but they also develop at an accelerated pace compared to ELLs who are literate but in another form of script.

ELLs who approach English literacy tasks with knowledge of another alphabetic system use this background knowledge. However, they need additional time and experiences with the Roman alphabet. Teachers should carefully consider the type and variety of fonts used in picture books to match the abilities of the ELLs. Picture books offer a variety of styles of fonts and can be selected for the purpose of giving ELLs experiences with them. For example, ELLs can benefit from reading a picture book written all in capital letters, or written in script. Familiarity with any alphabetic system, knowledge of the Roman alphabet, and strong educational backgrounds ease their transition to English. ELLs with the literacy skills closest to English progress at a faster pace. Others will progress according to the type and amount of literacy they bring to the task and the types and amounts of tasks they are given. Most ELLs benefit from engaging activities in which they practice connecting oral and written language. Some will also need to learn about the Roman alphabet itself.

Alphabet books can be found to meet the needs of children of all ages and to meet the needs of ELLs to learn different fonts, capital letters, and script. Two books written in capital letters are *Kente Colors* (Chocolte, 1996) and *Caveman: A B.C. Story* (Trasler, 2011). A book with its nouns written in capital letters is *A Cool Drink of Water* (Kerley, 2002). Two books written in script are *A Seed Is Sleepy* (Aston & Long, 2007) and *Night/Day: A Book of Eye-Catching Opposites* (Tullet, 1999). Aston and Long's book uses cursive script for its running text and manuscript print lettering for illustration labels.

Be aware of the difficulties posed by lack of familiarity with literacy or with the Roman alphabet, and select picture books accordingly. Select those books that are appropriate given the students' ages, literacy skills, and educational backgrounds. We must also consider their cultural backgrounds, since culture has a well-documented influence on second-language learning.

Culture

The importance of culture in language and in learning a second language cannot be ignored. Cultural aspects of a book can be a barrier to comprehension because they can add an unnecessary layer of content complexity. It is common practice in teaching English as a second language for the content of beginner classes to be universal concepts and palpable subjects. Using picture books with universal concepts and known topics will minimize the amount of information a beginner must process. When content is culturally familiar, ELLs can focus on language learning (Delpit, 2006; Kucer, 2009; Uso-Juan & Martinez-Flor, 2006). Book resources and book lists for ELLs are typically categorized by culture and culturally relevant topics (Hadaway, Vardell, & Young, 2002; Peregoy & Boyle, 2005). As with so many other aspects of selecting picture books, so much depends on who the students are and what they already know.

Contrasting two similar books with different cultural loads can help illustrate this. They are the wordless books about Carl the dog by Alexandra Day. The content of *Follow Carl* (1998) is basic and universal. The dog's owner and other children imitate the dog's antics as it jumps, runs, begs, rolls over, holds a stick, and leads the children. This content is transparently illustrated and easy to teach through gestures with total physical response (TPR). In contrast, the topic of *Carl Makes a Scrapbook* (1994) is culturally laden. A mischievous and fully humanized Carl fills a scrapbook with random photographs and memorabilia. Scrapbooking is not as universally familiar as the movements of *Follow Carl*, nor is it as amenable to teaching with gestures. The cultural content of these books makes one easier for ELLs to comprehend than the other.

Awareness of the difficulties posed by cultural content does not preclude teaching ELLs about cultural aspects of English and planning lessons to familiarize them with the new culture. In fact, picture books are useful in this regard. A particularly useful genre is the photographic essay of people around the world. Their photographs show cultural similarities as well as reflect cultural differences. ELLs learn English using the familiar photographs as a cultural reference upon which to build information about American and other cultures.

Another useful type of picture book is one that addresses a popular cultural topic. Picture books lend themselves to introducing ELLs to common American cultural and literary references, such as well-known story themes, characters, and narrative structures. Examples include the theme of feuding leading to tolerance and friendship between cats and dogs, the character of Cinderella, and the three-stage sequential structure found in such classics as *The Three Little Pigs* and *Goldilocks and the Three Bears*.

One of the wonderful things about picture books is that they cover a wide array of topics in a variety of ways. This allows for the flexibility needed to match books with students of different ages, languages, education levels, and cultural backgrounds. Their variety is an asset because books can be found to tap the knowledge and skills each ELL brings to English and to pace the introduction of new content so it is not overwhelming. In addition, the variety allows teachers to find books with features making them particularly useful for language learning.

2. HOW USEFUL IS THE CONTENT?

Useful content supports beginner ELLs in mastering the English used in and out of school. The ways picture books support the goal of learning English often mirror the strategies used by teachers of ELLs. The books present content with embedded verbal, visual, and experiential clues. Books with more of these clues or features are most useful, and those with fewer clues are less so. When beginner ELLs use books with these features, their language development accelerates because they comprehend the message and have models for expression and interaction. These books are a scaffold for English and for school subjects. Three different types support second-language learning: books with socially oriented formats, books with obvious topic organization, and thematic books.

Social Orientation

Many picture books are socially oriented rather than content oriented. They are embedded with features typical of oral exchanges and thus interactively engage the reader. These built-in verbal, visual, and experiential devices provide a contextually rich situation. They call on the reader to actively respond to something or identify personally with a main character, often an animal with anthropomorphic characteristics. The formats guide readers into an exchange with the author, illustrator, or others experiencing the book.

These types of books are useful in teaching English communicative competency. As they experience the book, ELLs develop powerful foundational language skills because they are exposed to an interactive language situation. The books provide examples of the English used by English speakers to exchange basic information, such as general vocabulary and sentence structures. The books create venues for ELLs to master linguistic competency, such as the subsystems of phonology, morphology, and syntax, as well as other communicative competencies. The venue teaches ELLs basic words, such as those referred to as Tier 1 words and those on the General Service List (GSL). The books create opportunities for ELLs to learn these words in context, such as when the word is part of a formulaic phrase, in a question, or in a basic sentence pattern. Exposing ELLs to different formats of socially oriented books teaches them to use these words across social contexts. For example, a question pattern used in an interactive text, in which readers find answers in the pictures, could be applicable to a guessing game or to the inquiry required in a science task.

The language taught with these books is that used in everyday social situations. It helps ELLs learn to compare, inquire, and problem-solve in English with undemanding, here-and-now content. This is a good foundation for the type of English used in school situations with more sophisticated content. Picture books are useful as an introduction to basic vocabulary and syntax and as a way to transition to academic English. For example, ELLs become familiar with the names of basic concepts, such as words for numbers in mathematics, countries in geography, and natural elements in science. They also are exposed to the syntactic structures in which these names occur, such as in a question or in a paragraph with common signal words for sequence, coherence, and cohesion. These books can be used as a resource to prepare ELLs by easing the linguistic load before having to compare, inquire about, and problem-solve in mathematics, science, and social studies.

A good example of a socially oriented picture book is a songbook. While some picture books are compilations of several songs, others contain only one. A single-song book enhances comprehension by providing robust illustrations for every line of the song. Such books also contain many embedded scaffolds leading to extra practice of expression and fluency because they have repetitive lines, musical scores, and promote unison experiences with classmates.[1] Two examples of songbooks that are beautifully illustrated and appeal to school-aged ELLs are *Let It Shine: Three Favorite Spirituals* by the Coretta Scott King Award–winning illustrator Ashley Bryan (2007) and *Joseph Had a Little Overcoat* (Taback, 1999), a Caldecott Medal book.

In addition songbooks, books about artwork and crafts are particularly easy to use with all age groups to promote language learning through interaction. Masterpieces of art and the use of crafts are subjects that appeal to the sophisticated abilities of high school ELLs. Again, the content is important, but so too is the interactive nature of the experience, which provides for language learning and helps the earliest level beginner to practice using Tier 1 and GSL words. A good number of books about artwork and crafts require ELLs to learn the names of objects, animals, numbers, colors, and shapes. A few will also provide opportunities for learning the language of more sophisticated concepts. Included in the discussions that follow are examples of easy books for learning to compare objects visually as well as books with more complex English, such as poems using similes.

Books with basic concepts that are illustrated with masterpieces of art are ideally suited to teaching beginner ELLs of all grades because the illustrations are not babyish but sophisticated. For example, Micklethwait's *I Spy Shapes in Art* (2004) presents basic geometry terms by having readers find them in masterpieces. Her *I Spy Two Eyes: Numbers in Art* (1998) does the same in presenting numbers. Two art books presenting basic phrases are *Oooh! Picasso* (Niepold & Verdu, 2009) and *Oooh! Matisse* (Niepold & Verdu, 2007). Both have guessing game formats and thus encourage use of the language used in interactions.

In addition to books about masterpieces of art, books about crafts are particularly well suited to teaching ELLs of all grades. They are useful in implementing cooperative learning. Cooperative learning is beneficial to language learning because it presents language in a venue replete with scaffolds, everything from social feedback to manipulatives, to natural pauses for processing, to integrated presentation of oral and written forms. Books about craft projects provide visual clues to meaning and occasions for interactions, as students help each other complete each step.

Crafts are represented in picture books in a variety of formats. Some books are visually the results of different types of artistic media and can be used as models for ELLs. For example, a book of paper collages or photographs of clay figures provides readers with models they can use for illustrating their own books. Other books contain explicit directions. ELLs benefit from having models of the sentence and discourse structures used to give directions.

Picture books about paper crafts are ideal for teaching ELLs. They provide opportunities for extra language practice. For example, ELLs can identify illustrations and review the sequential steps. A number of examples of paper-craft picture books are illustrated entirely with geometric shapes. Ehlert's *Color Zoo* (1989a) and *Color Farm* (1990) consist of labeled geometric shapes that are made into animal illustrations. They are a springboard for ELLs of all ages to use words related to mathematics, animals, and art. Emberley's *Ed Emberley's Picture Pie Two* (2005b) and *Ed Emberley's Picture*

Pie (2006f) also consist of labeled geometric shapes. Emberley's books focus on the circle and have an explicit instructional format. His books can be used for teaching such mathematical concepts as addition of fractions and calculation of area. Hall's *My Heart Is Like a Zoo* (2010) contains more text and language arts content. Each animal is made with parts of heart shapes and is accompanied by a simile about emotions and feelings. Again, each of these books presents upper grade ELLs with age appropriate content and plenty of opportunities for engaging in learning English through interaction. In addition to these, several other types are particularly well suited to the needs of upper grade ELLs.

Socially Oriented Books for Upper Grade ELLs

Upper grade beginner ELLs are able to engage in a wider range of social interactions than younger ELLs because of their more sophisticated cognitive abilities, content knowledge, interests, and language skills. These students are able to use one or several books as springboards for language- and content-focused learning. In fact, they fulfill a need for guided experiences with the academic language of schools. Picture books are ideal for teaching them to compare and contrast content, genres, and deeper truths. For example, upper grade beginners can use a book to examine a sophisticated truth, such as an allegorical tale about tolerance. They can also use it as a template for writing a book of their own and work in groups as they personalize a version to reflect their ideas, backgrounds, cultures, and the intended readers.

Age makes it possible for upper grade beginners to engage in language-focused academic activities using several books or sources of information. Examples of picture books with several sources of factual information are a series of books by Thomas Locker about natural phenomena. *Mountain Dance* (2001) and *Water Dance* (2002) contain English within the beginner ELP range. In each book, natural elements are presented poetically in the running text with a painting, and in end pages with expository text. The format lends itself to teaching about poetic devices as well as the language of inquiry through comparing the different types of text, content, and sources of information.

Finally, the relative sophistication of upper grade ELLs helps them create opportunities for working together in groups on book-based projects without the teacher, even when they are at an early beginner stage. For example, they can plan a book-based project by accessing multiple resources, such as digital media about a book's topic. Picture books for such book-based projects include those that can be performed, such as a poem or dramatic story. Two such books are Langston Hughes' poem *My*

People (2009a) and Shane Evans's dramatic yet minimalistic story about the Underground Railroad, *Underground: Finding the Light to Freedom* (2011). Evans's story is also an example of another type of useful book, one with transparent organization.

Topic Organization

Books with obvious topic organization are ideal for beginner ELLs. We want books with organizational features promoting comprehension, expression, language-focused learning, and fluency. These books provide opportunities for teaching content because content words and frequently used academic vocabulary are best understood within a conceptual framework. A text's organization and discourse structure provide examples for ELLs and can be used to introduce this language with an easy everyday topic before it is used in an academic text. Frequently used organization in picture books includes orderly sequencing and the use of paratext.

Texts containing explicit sequential devices are the easiest for beginners. Sequential supports frequently found in picture books include formulaic phrases for sequence, explicit story summaries in end pages, maps reviewing events, and time lines. The use of these reduces the cognitive load, allowing ELLs to focus on new language and content.

Paratext is another organizational device. *Paratext* refers to the elements surrounding the main text. Examples of typical paratext in picture books are labeled illustrations, speech bubbles, asides, front matter, and end page notes to parents or teachers. These are not the only forms of paratext. A good number of picture books use paratext elements similar to those of textbooks. For example, they contain subtitles, tables of content, section headings, glossaries, and graphic summaries.

These types of paratext provide important scaffolds for ELLs. They help ELLs access content concepts and language meaning. They are useful in applying an important communicative language teaching (CLT) strategy, the preteaching of key vocabulary (Calderon, 2007). For example, ELLs can identify key vocabulary in an index, table of contents, or glossary. These can be explicitly taught before ELLs are confused by encountering them in running text alongside less important information.

Simplification devices specific to the picturebook medium are also helpful in teaching ELLs. One example is when a picture book separates books for each subsection of a larger topic rather then dividing a concept's subtopics into chapters of one book. Another is when a picture book illustrates key concepts with tiny pictures on the inside cover rather than in an alphabetical index in the end pages.

Thus, a variety of picture book text elements provide ELLs with opportunities for language learning. Those features favoring social interaction and obvious organization of concepts are of great benefit to ELLs. They provide opportunities for recursive exposures to new vocabulary and many opportunities for deep processing of these words as they occur in sentences and are used in context. ELLs benefit from encountering the same topic in a wide variety of formats and genres. The final topic in discussing the utility of content is themes. Gathering books by themes is an ideal way to accelerate ELP development.

Themes

Picture book resources for beginner ELLs should note book themes. As was seen in Chapter 1 with books about butterflies, immersing ELLs in a theme benefits language learning. It creates opportunities for sustained practice of topical vocabulary used with a variety of books and activities. The repeated encounters develop a deep knowledge of English morphology and syntax. The increased familiarity with the topic lessens the ELLs' processing load, and they move beyond a focus on comprehension to focus on developing expression, fluency, and language knowledge.

This book's appendix includes tellable books listed by themes in order to help plan units revolving around topics. The themes are listed in the following paragraphs. For practical reasons, only a few more than a dozen themes are used. The first reason for selection of these themes reflects the fact that picture books have a limited range of topics.

The second reason reflects the needs of ELLs. It is easiest to plan units around popular picture book topics because there is enough quantity from which to select several books to fully explore a subject. Good themes for beginner ELLs are those with a dozen or more books, of different types, that all adhere to tellability criteria. For example, the most prevalent theme by far is animals. The reasons for this are not germane to the purposes of this book, except as an explanation. There are so many books about animals that I divide them into smaller subthemes, such as farm animals, pets, cats, and tiny animals.

A third reason for the choice of themes presented in this book reflects the nature of picture books. Picture book authors have their own creative reasons for their choices of topics and their presentation. These differ significantly from those of academic texts (Lemke, 1998; Sipe, 1998). In general, most picture books represent content according to categories quite different from those used in school textbooks. For example, animals in picture books are not grouped using standard scientific classifications or scientific nomenclature to distinguish insects, spiders, bugs, and worms.

Instead, as part of appealing to young children, picture books might group these by their small size, their being newborn, or the types of sounds they make.

As a result of the limited availability and types of themes in picture books and the needs of beginner ELLs, books with tellability are grouped into general themes. These are listed below beginning with animals, because the list is in alphabetical order, and animals represent the largest theme found in picture books. As mentioned above, within the animal theme, there are many subthemes with an abundant number of books, such as tiny animals and pets.

Another frequent theme of picture books is people. People books occur in all types and genres, and they include books about people around the world, families, and celebrations. Among the many books about people, the largest includes fictional animal tales and books that are in essence about people but are illustrated with animal characters. In the lists in this book, these books are not included under the larger people theme but are instead found with books about friendship. A good number of friendship-themed animal stories are parables, fables, and allegories. These are useful with all age groups.

Other than these two large themes, animals and people, the appendix and the list that follows label themes in accordance with groupings used by many other book lists, such as crafts, food, humor, transportation, and others associated with the four academic areas mathematics, science, social studies, and language arts. Each theme contains more than a dozen books, in a variety of formats, different genres, and ELP levels.

The themes are as follows:

- Animals. When relevant, animal books are labeled as part of a sub-theme, such as farm animals, pets, and tiny animals. Most pet-themed books are about cats and dogs. Tiny animals include bugs, insects, spiders, worms, et cetera.
- Concepts. When relevant, concept books will be listed with the name of the concept itself, such as ABCs, clothes, or colors.
- Crafts and art.
- Food.
- Fiction and language arts.
- Friendship. This theme includes animal parables, fables, and allegories, such as books about cooperation and tolerance.
- Humor.
- Mathematics. When relevant, mathematics books are labeled with subthemes, such as counting, shapes, and measurement.
- Music. This includes folklore and songs.

- People. Subthemes include families and celebrations.
- Science. When relevant, science subthemes are labeled, such as nature, plants, and space.
- Social Studies. When relevant, subthemes are listed, such as geography and history.
- Time. When relevant, subthemes are listed, such as weather, seasons, days of the week, and months.
- Transportation includes books about vehicles and travel.

In the end, the utility of a theme is defined broadly. The particular themes listed above are found in a number of books with tellability. They provide ELLs with recursive exposure to vocabulary and a variety of sentence structures. Other themes are just as useful, but as of the writing of this book, they have fewer numbers of books.

Teachers will find that having a large group of books on a theme, while useful, is not required for planning second-language learning activities. There are tellable picture books that address topics not listed above. They may have many features compatible with the needs of ELLs. For example, a book containing lots of WH questions (who? what? where? why? which? when? how?) can be used to supplement a unit on a theme regardless of whether its content is thematic. Once ELLs master the WH question form, they can transfer this skill to asking questions about the thematic books. Thus, the importance of a book's content is weighed against a number of considerations. One of the most important considerations and the last of the three questions used to explore content difficulty is whether the book is interesting to ELLs.

3. HOW INTERESTING IS THE BOOK'S CONTENT?

A student's interest in a book has profound consequences for learning (Garcia & Beltran, 2003). Motivation and personal connections to topics create precisely the type of sustained practice a beginner needs (Cienchanowski, 2009).[2] Students reread the books more often and have better long-term recall of information.

Their interest in books can be used as a motivator to learn the everyday words needed to describe actions, feelings, desires, needs, and objects—words listed on the GSL. They may also be interested in learning the academic words used across subjects to express relationships among concepts—words listed on the Academic Word List (AWL). In addition, these books help them participate in subject-specific tasks. They want to learn the language of science, social studies, language arts, and mathematics.

Science

Informational picture books about science are ideal for teaching concepts and skills to ELLs who would be overwhelmed by books about the same subject with fewer contextual cues. The books expose ELLs to the multiple representations used in science books, such as the use of photographic evidence, diagrams, flowcharts, graphs, inserts, and matrixes (de Oliveira, Hadaway, & Mundy, 2010). ELLs learn the language used to refer to these representations as well as to the concepts they represent, such as taxonomy, classification, and cause and effect.

Two popular books by award-winning author/illustrators about animals illustrate the use of science-related thinking: *What Do You Do With a Tail Like This?* (Page & Jenkins, 2003) for older ELLs, and for younger ones, *Who Hops?* (Davis, 2001). *Who Hops?* consists of transparently organized patterned questions and answers about a particular mode of movement, such as slithering, swimming, or hopping. The title establishes the question pattern, which is repeated throughout with other verbs. Each question is followed by examples that readers can use as a classification activity based on movement. For each verb, there are several true examples and one humorous nonexample; for example, a nonexample would be a cow flying. Each nonexample is followed by a clear negation indicating this animal cannot do this movement.

What Do You Do With a Tail Like This? uses the same rhetorical device. Its title question establishes an inquiry pattern that is repeated throughout with other body parts, such as ears and mouths. The book is more linguistically challenging, both in amount and complexity, than *Who Hops?* Consequently, it requires ELLs to be able to learn more precise and academically oriented terminology. Additionally, it contains samples of science paratext, such as diagrams and matrixes.

Social Studies

Social studies picture books can interest students who are curious about the United States as well as other cultures. Through award-winning picture books, they can learn the language needed to participate in lessons on geography, history, and cultural topics (Glandon, 2000c). One way picture books capture their interest is by using common social studies devices, such as maps, time lines, cultural artifacts, and folklore. Some books capture their interest on an emotional level; for example, upper grade ELLs will connect with freedom stories, such as the earlier mentioned book by Shane Evans about the Underground Railroad, and a book by Joseph Slate, *I Want to Be Free* (2009).

One of the simplest books for introducing an American map is *Wow! America!* (Neubecker, 2006). Each of the book's regional maps includes illustrations of famous things of the area. Another book about American geography is *This Land Is Your Land* (Guthrie & Jakobsen, 2002). The text comprises the popular song lyrics, and the illustrations follow a westward journey across the United States.

By far, some of the most interesting social studies books for ELLs are those that include familiar people and cultures. There is a small genre of picture books known as photographic essays. Most of these books are about people around the world and are written to contain parallel information about each. Again, as mentioned before, ELLs can easily refer to them while learning to describe, compare, and contrast information. These books provide an additional support for teaching ELLs the language of description, comparison, and contrast because they contain two types of text. First, the photographs are accompanied by sparse narrative or poetic text, and second, the end pages are expository. This expository end page text describes the location of each photograph; it's a sort of photographic index. Many of these books also include a map with locations of each photograph marked.

Three examples of these are *Bread, Bread, Bread* (1993a) from a series by Ann Morris, *A Cool Drink of Water* (2002) from a National Geographic Society series by Barbara Kerley, and *Carrying* (1999a) from the Small World series by Gwenyth Swain. The last is a treasure for teachers seeking bilingual books for languages from across the globe.

Language Arts

Many picture books connect to language arts content. They represent a wide variety of genres, story elements, and literary devices and are a vast resource for introducing students to language arts (Glandon, 2000a; Hall, 2001, 2007; Van Zile & Napoli, 2009). Two of the most prevalent genres are stories and concept books. Popular stories come in a host of different versions, including some that will capture the interest of older students. For example, versions of *The Three Little Pigs* abound. Concept books can be highly sophisticated and be interesting for different age groups. An example of a high-concept alphabet book would be *Bembo's Zoo: An Animal ABC Book* (De Vicq de Cumptich, 2000), because it uses letters to make the images of each animal.

Literary devices are abundant in picture books. Of course, the simpler ones are most prevalent, for example, repetition, rhyme, parallelism, and hyperbole. Examples of books that use hyperbole are *My Dad* (Browne, 2001) and *My Mom* (Browne, 2009). Examples of short poems with sophisticated literary devices such as metaphor for upper grade ELLs are *Rooster/Gallo*, a bilingual verse by Lujan and Monroy (2004) and *My People* by Langston Hughes (2009a). Finally, also for middle and high school–aged students, is a book of haiku using a variety of poetic devices, Raczka's *Guyku: A Year of Haiku for Boys* (2010). Examples from this book are available online at www.guykuhaiku.com.

Mathematics

Picture books on mathematical topics include concepts presented visually and verbally (Leuenberger, 2007). Most often, the representation of a content topic assumes readers' ability to think critically given their age. Simple concepts, such as counting from one to ten, assume a young audience. But it is difficult to find books with easy English and yet mathematical concepts or problems that are appropriate for older students. The earlier discussion of books about crafts included some with geometrical shapes that lend themselves to introducing fractions, such as *Ed Emberley's Picture Pie* (2006f) and *Picture Pie Two* (2005b).

Some picture books introduce mathematics topics connected to familiar subjects. For example, students fascinated with kitchen mathematics will enjoy books with recipes, such as *What's Cookin'?* (Coffelt, 2003). Students interested in art can learn numbers by searching for the numerals 1 through 20 in masterpieces of art in *I Spy Two Eyes: Numbers in Art* (Micklethwait, 1998).

CONCLUSION

An underlying concept of CLT is "less is more." For ELLs, experiencing books with minimal language has profound benefits on their ELP progress. They can deeply process the limited text, because it is accompanied by visual and other scaffolds in a supportive social context. In Chapter 1, this concept was applied to finding picture books covering the basics of a balanced CLT program, that is, teaching comprehension, expression, language-focused learning, and fluency.

In this chapter, the concept was applied to finding books with the right content for school-aged ELLs. Books that demand less cognitive effort reduce the cognitive load on ELLs. This provides ELLs with more opportunities to build communicative skills, and this in turn accelerates language development.

In sum, books with tellability are those with content that is familiar and easy for ELLs. Finding a useful, interesting, or accessible book requires considering the ELLs' age, literacy, education, and cultural background. ELLs' interest in a book is a key factor in their ability to understand content and in the amount of effort they will put into learning from book-based activities.

This chapter on finding books with the right content would not be complete without reference to Cummins's description of the interplay between context, content, and language. In terms of content, tellable books are those that make few cognitive demands. In terms of language, they contain contextual scaffolds. Finding books with this type of language is explored in the next chapters.

TELLABILITY IN PRACTICE: USING CONTENT CRITERIA

First, select one of the books listed in Box 2.2 and analyze it according to the concepts discussed in the chapter. Next, select a book from your classroom, library, or bookstore, and analyze it in the same way.

Consider content, language, and student characteristics in answering the following questions:

2.1. How difficult or demanding is the content?

2.2. How useful is it?

2.3. How interesting and relevant is it?

Box 2.2   Alphabetical List of Titles Cited in Chapter 2

Topic: Animals

Bembo's Zoo: An Animal ABC Book (de Vicq de Cumptich, 2000) uses letters to make animal illustrations.

Carl Makes a Scrapbook (Day, 1994) and *Follow Carl* (Day, 1998) have wordless, sequential plots.

Color Zoo (Ehlert, 1989a) and *Color Farm* (Ehlert, 1990) illustrate using geometric shapes.

Ed Emberley's Picture Pie (Emberley, 2006f) and *Picture Pie Two* (Emberley, 2005b) use geometric shapes to teach illustration.

How Many Birds Flew Away? A Counting Book With a Difference (Giganti & Crews, 2005) contains arithmetic.

Rooster/Gallo (Lujan & Monroy, 2004) uses metaphor.

What Do You Do With a Tail Like This? (Jenkins & Page, 2003) describes animal attributes.

Who Hops? (Davis, 2001) describes animal movements.

Topic: People

Caveman: A B.C. Story (Trasler, 2011) uses capital letters.

How Much, How Many, How Far, How Heavy, How Long, How Tall Is 1000? (Nolan, 1995) measures and quantifies.

Guyku: A Year of Haiku for Boys (Raczka, 2010) uses poetic devices, including humor.

I Spy Two Eyes: Numbers in Art (Micklethwait, 1998) contains numerals embedded in works of art.

(Continued)

(Continued)

> *I Want to Be Free* (Slate, 2009) appeals emotionally because of a strong main character.
>
> *Joseph Had a Little Overcoat* (Taback, 1999) contains musical score to sing.
>
> *Kente Colors* (Chocolte, 1996) uses capital letters.
>
> *Let It Shine* (Bryan, 2007) contains three folk songs with their musical score.
>
> *My Dad* (Browne, 2001) and *My Mom* (Browne, 2009) use parallelism, simile, and hyperbole.
>
> *My People* (Hughes, 2009a) uses metaphor.
>
> *This Land Is Your Land* (Guthrie & Jakobsen, 2002) uses U.S. maps with landmarks and song.
>
> *Underground: Finding the Light to Freedom* (Evans, 2011) uses intense and minimalistic dramatic text.
>
> *What's Cookin'?* (Coffelt, 2003) applies kitchen mathematics.
>
> *Wow! America!* (Neubecker, 2006) uses U.S. maps with landmarks.

Other Topics

Mountain Dance (Locker, 2001) and *Water Dance* (Locker, 2002) integrates subjects.

Night/Day: A Book of Eye-Catching Opposites (Tullet, 1999) uses script.

Oooh! Picasso (Niepold &Verdu, 2009) has interactive text about sculptures.

A Seed Is Sleepy (Aston, 2007) uses script in text and manuscript for labels.

NOTES

1. See the website of the Center for Applied Linguistics at http://www.cal.org/resources/digest/singable.html for a list of singable books by Betty A. Smallwood (2008).

2. Additional resources for using picture books with content include Blake-Pearson's (2005) book about using picture books with older learners and Bowman-Perrott, Herrera, and Murry's (2010) lists of content text challenges.

3 Selecting Books With the Right Language Input

By definition, a book with tellability accelerates English language proficiency (ELP) development because its text matches the instructional range of the English language learner (ELL). These books consistently create opportunities for ELLs to succeed in book-based interactions. Conversely, books that are above their ELP are too challenging, and those below their ELP are too easy. The teacher must mediate between these books and the student's abilities. Finding the right book requires matching text to students' ELP.

Current book lists for ELLs are a good place to start a search for a book with the right ELP level. These lists contain books that are grouped by generally accepted ELP levels. However, these ELP levels are broadly defined. Particularly for beginner ELLs, these levels represent too wide a range for teachers to be able to closely match students to texts. For early beginners, most of the books are too hard, and for productive beginners, some are too easy.

When books match different stages of beginners, language learning flows, and improvement is measurable. For example, the earliest beginner, who is usually silent, easily joins in choral activities when the text is repetitive. The emergent beginner, who usually uses a one-word response, engages in guessing games based on a text containing question-and-answer routines. The productive beginner will use a book with an obvious plot as a template for writing a personalized story. Each of these books matched a beginner in a different stage of beginner language development. In order to match books to stages of within the beginner level, we need a more nuanced description of the linguistic challenge. As was seen in

Chapter 2, Cummins's work provides a useful place to start categorizing beginner picture books (see Box 2.1 on p. 15). Picture books for beginners fall into Quadrant A because they contain contextually embedded language and cognitively undemanding content. Picture books in Quadrant A can be further divided into narrower stages that match books to beginners' instructional abilities.

Unfortunately, linguistic difficulty is a complex construct encompassing a considerable number of factors. Fortunately, we can organize beginner picture books into four stages of difficulty based on a few key ones. These are length, complexity, and utility of the text. Length is important because beginners can only process so much at one time. Complexity of the vocabulary and structures will increase the amount of processing. We also must consider the style of a text because useful language and language that is frequently encountered are easier to learn. An example of the easiest texts would be a book that is short in terms of total running words, has simple sentences, and contains a high number of useful interactive phrases. In contrast, a text with the opposite qualities contains much more linguistic load and thus is more difficult to process. These key variables provide enough information about the language in a book to answer the essential question of whether the text is too difficult, too easy, or just right. All three will be explored in the following sections, and utility is further described in Chapter 5.

DIFFICULTY OF THE TEXT

Traditional measures of text difficulty provide standard and useful information for exploring a text's difficulty. The best known are readability measures and leveled book formulas (August & Shanahan, 2005; Fountas & Pinnell, 2005; Fry, 2002). These measures take into account a combination of language variables with high correlation to overall text difficulty. The three most frequent variables included in these measures are word length, average number of words in a sentence, and total number of words in the sample. These text-bound variables are often coupled with other book features, such as associations between text and accompanying illustrations. In addition to these tangible text and illustration variables, we should consider ones outside the books themselves, such as the students and context (Harris & Hodges, 1995; Nation, 2001). The accuracy of any measure increases when it includes student and situational variables. As was discussed in previous chapters, these types of variables are, in fact, basic to searching for the right book for beginner ELLs. Difficulty depends on the critical student variables of age, educational background, and ELP and on the situation in which language learning is taking place (Hiebert & Kamil, 2005; Richard-Amato & Snow, 2005; Rost, 2006). For example, all beginner

ELLs will find books with repetitive vocabulary easy to learn. Beginners who are older and have stronger educational backgrounds can learn the same amount in a comparatively shorter time.

In addition to the age and background factors making the vocabulary easy, vocabulary difficulty also depends on context. Some picture books present vocabulary with more linguistic redundancy than others. Linguistic redundancy is broadly described as the interplay of various integrated linguistic subsystems that together communicate meaning. One small example of redundancy would be the plurals in the phrase *there are two books.* It is expressed in the word *are,* the word *two,* and by a suffix—*s.* Linguistic redundancies occur across oral and written morphological, phonological, syntactic, and discourse subsystems. A book with a maximum amount of redundancy is easier than one that is dense. The earliest stage beginner needs a maximum amount of text redundancy, and each later stage beginner needs less.

Using the following three criteria provides enough information to capture key linguistic, student, and situational variables to organize beginner picture books into useful categories of linguistic difficulty:

1. Amount of Language. This refers to the total amount of words, the total amount of unknown words, and the ratio of known to unknown words.

2. Linguistic Complexity. This refers to the difficulty of the book's text, such as the types of vocabulary and sentences.

3. Utility. This refers to the redundancy of the text as used in a language learning context.

Together these criteria help categorize books by answering two basic questions: How much text is there and how difficult is the language? and How useful is it for language learning? This chapter addresses these questions. (Chapter 5 provides much more detailed answers to the question of utility because it describes ways to match texts' styles to particular communicative language teaching [CLT] strategies.)

How long and how difficult is the text?

Using the interplay of the first two criteria, amount and complexity, beginner books can be organized into the following four stages:

- Stage 1, short and simple text.
- Stage 2, longer yet simple text.
- Stage 3, short yet complex text.
- Stage 4, longer and more complex text.

Stage 1 books are easiest because there are minimal numbers of new words and total words in the running text. The language consists of distinguishable sound patterns, easy vocabulary, short sentences, and an obvious discourse structure. Stage 2 books have more text but are still relatively simple. For example, a Stage 2 book may be repetitious, increasing the length but making the number of new words small. Stage 3 books contain more complexity than those in Stages 1 and 2, although they are not necessarily longer. In Stage 4 books, both amount and complexity increase.

The following matrix summarizes these stages.

Box 3.1 Stages of Beginner-Level Picture Books	
Stage 1. Books with a minimal amount of text, a minimal number of running words, and fewer than 20 new words to learn. These books contain salient and simple linguistic elements and patterns.	**Stage 2.** Books with more running text than those in Stage 1. These books still contain fewer than 20 new words and are simple linguistically.
Stage 3. Books that still have a limited number of running words but that include a wider range of vocabulary and sentence structures, reflecting more complexity than Stage 2 books.	**Stage 4.** Books with incrementally more complexity and text than books at the first three stages.

The pertinence of having four stages can be illustrated with one example, *Jack's Garden* (Cole, 1995), a book with appropriate content (planting a garden) and language for school-aged beginner ELLs. (The patterned text is accompanied by beautiful whole-page illustrations.) This book contains three different types of text; each matches a different stage of beginner.

The number of new words in the running text is within the range of an early beginner stage. Stage 1 books will introduce no more than 20 new words (Nation, 2001, 2008). (This number fluctuates down to accommodate earlier developmental ages.) This book introduces about 25 concrete verbs and nouns. More or less, a new pair of vocabulary words occurs in a patterned phrase on each page using the cumulative format of the well-known folktale, "This Is the House That Jack Built." For example, *garden* and *planted* are introduced on the first page, and *soil* and *made up* are introduced on the next page. Each page repeats the previous content words and adds two more. The words that need to be explicitly taught are concrete concepts, such as *rain, insects, flowers, sipped, fell*, and *wet.*

The amount of language in a text also includes the total number of words, the text's length, and the ratio of known to unknown words (Nation, 2001, 2008). *Jack's Garden* has about 250 running words, and thus a ratio of 25 new words to 250 total words. This makes it pedagogically sound for beginners. This ratio is achieved because of the cumulative sentence structure. Although the ELLs encounter an ever-increasing amount of text per page, there is a limited number of new words. This type of repetitive, sequential, and cumulative discourse structure is easy to understand and promotes language learning.

Jack's Garden is also interesting in terms of linguistic complexity. While the vocabulary is easy, the syntax might be judged to be complex because the tale is told in one long complex sentence. But, in fact, the difficulty of the sentence is reduced because of its redundancies. It has a repetitious syntactic pattern, and each new clause appears on a new page. The long complex sentence is parsed across many illustrated pages. In sum, based on the amount of language, and its simplicity, the running text would fall into Stage 2.

This is not, however, a full picture of the linguistic challenges and opportunities of this book. *Jack's Garden*, like so many picture books, also contains additional texts. One is a set of labeled illustrations and the other an expository end page. Both require more linguistic processing because they introduce new vocabulary and discourse styles. The labeled illustrations introduce some 100 more vocabulary items, such as names of specific birds and insects. These require more linguistic processing because they appear without the contextual support provided by a patterned sentence.

The book's end pages have roughly the same number of words as the running text, about 250. However, unlike the repetitious and patterned running text, the end pages contain substantially more new vocabulary. The words are introduced in a comparatively more dense and academic written style. These other texts would fall into Stage 4.

This analysis of the critical variables in *Jack's Garden* illustrates the benefits of examining a text's linguistic load. In this case, the running text is within the range of early beginners, while the other texts fall within a later stage. Each of these texts also differs in terms of its utility for language learning.

Is it useful for language learning?

As was illustrated above with *Jack's Garden*, matching texts to the ELP range of students involves examining the amount and complexity of the book's language. It also involves examining whether the text lends itself to different types of language learning activities. First, ELLs benefit from books that develop foundational language skills used in everyday social interactions. Second, ELLs, particularly those in upper grades, need books that introduce and develop academic language skills. Third, they need books that provide opportunities to develop communicative competency, which is the ability to know when, where, and how to use language across contexts.

Jack's Garden lends itself to teaching all three. Basic social language can be learned through unison activities with its patterned text. Developing communicative competency is supported in that it lends itself to a cooperative gardening project. Academic language can be introduce through the science content. Finally, the additional texts lend themselves to language-focused study.

LANGUAGE-FOCUSED STUDY FOR UPPER GRADE ELLS

Upper grade ELLs can use *Jack's Garden* with explicit vocabulary learning strategies. The labeled illustrations are like a picture dictionary and can be used for explicit vocabulary learning tasks. These labeled illustrations are organized semantically. For example, a page might focus on birds, insects, or garden tools. They are a resource for such tasks as categorizing, matching, sorting, and word association. Upper grade ELLs can study the way they reflect science concepts, such as life cycles, interdependency in nature, and classification of small animals.

The illustrated words can be used in a common vocabulary learning strategy, substitution. For example, ELLs can substitute the labeled words for the same parts of speech in the running text. This requires paying attention to the rules for pluralizing. For example, a labeled word is singular, *bluebird,* and the word to be substituted in the running text is plural, *birds.*

The different text formats are useful in language-focused study of discourse devices, for example, comparing the end notes to the poetic text. The end notes can be used as a model for paragraph writing. It contains standard devices for coherence and cohesion, such as the use of parallel sentences as first sentences of paragraphs.

Finally, the book's multiple texts expose the ELLs to a variety of language experiences. ELLs benefit from recursive encounters with each text structure. Four different and useful types of texts are found among picture books on the plant theme included in the following section. These linguistic structures are the following:

1. Texts about projects, for example texts with the language of commands, directives, and procedures, such as the steps to growing plants, making crafts, or conducting kitchen mathematics (such as cooking vegetables).

2. Fiction, for example, books with sequential structures and other literary devices.

3. Expository texts, for example, books with academic language and with paratext useful for vocabulary-focused language learning strategies.

4. Poetic texts, for example, books containing poetic devices, features compatible with developing oral fluency, and features for making connections between oral and written styles.

I end this chapter by briefly describing a few books about gardening organized by stages of beginner linguistic difficulty (see Box 3.2). Also included are a few high utility books. The books have tellability—they adhere to CLT principles, have undemanding content, are grouped according to stages of beginner ELP, and include the four types of text.

STAGE 1: SHORT AND SIMPLE BOOKS FOR SILENT BEGINNERS

Stage 1 books contain small amounts of new language presented in simple patterns. The sparse text contains fewer than 20 words or variants of words to be learned. They are short enough to be reread deliberately and with frequent pauses several times in a lesson. The level of vocabulary addresses the needs of beginners for basic words, such as numbers, nouns, and verbs used every day, like *carry, pick, water,* and *grow.* They also include basic and recurring words on the gardening theme, such as *flower, leaf, root, seed, soil,* and *stem.*

The book *Ten Seeds* (Brown, 2001b) is an example. It consists of simple noun phrases that refer to subtracting by one, such as "ten seeds" becomes "nine seeds." The word *one* is repeated 10 times, making it 25% of the total running words. The book can be taught with repetitive unison activities. A Spanish version, *Diez Semillas* (Brown, 2001a) can be used to improve comprehension. Older ELLs can tap their background linguistic knowledge and engage in the explicit language learning strategy, comparing and contrasting.

Stage 1 books are within the range of the earliest beginner ELLs. The book is a springboard to learning "here and now" language, such as affirming and negating facts, using plural and singular, and following simple directions.

The following are four additional examples of alphabetically listed Stage 1 books:

Green Starts: In the Garden (IKids, 2009) has short, simple sentences. Its back page has information on growing a garden that lends itself to the language experience approach (LEA) strategy.

My Garden/Mi Jardín (Emberley, 2008) has 20 bilingually (Spanish/English) labeled illustrations of concrete objects that can also be sorted such as *dirt, shovel, hose,* and *watering can.* Its bilingual text is useful for comprehension. Older ELLs can engage in the language learning strategy compare and contrast.

Pumpkin, Pumpkin (Titherington, 1986) is the simple, sequential story of the plant's life cycle. It lends itself to the strategy titled retelling.

Up, Down, and Around (Ayres, 2007) has several sets of patterned couplets about the way vegetables grow; for example, broccoli grows up above ground while beets grow below. It lends itself to using the language teaching strategies reenactment and realia.

STAGE 2: LONGER, SIMPLE BOOKS FOR EMERGENT BEGINNERS

Stage 2 books contain an increased number of concrete nouns, verbs, and adjectives but not much more complexity. The increase in length is often a result of linguistic redundancies, such as repetitive and patterned words, phrases, and text structure. I place into this stage books with more than 20 new words and word variants to be taught. Some of the books may have upwards of 50 concrete nouns, adjectives, and verbs because we can assume that by the time ELLs are learning with Stage 2 books, some of these have been taught.

The book *The Carrot Seed* (Kraus, 1988) is an example. The simple story is patterned and has repetition with about 100 total running words. The 1996 Spanish version, *La Semilla De Zanahoria,* can be used to increase comprehension and learning through comparing and contrasting languages.

Stage 2 books are within the range of ELLs who can process more amounts of language. ELLs use them to respond to simple book-based directives of a wider range. They engage in simple expressive activities, such as retelling and reader's theater. The following are more examples of Stage 2 books:

Flower Garden (Bunting, 2000) serves as a template for making a flower box garden. The bilingual Spanish/English version, *Flower Garden / Jardín de Flores* (1994) can be used to increase comprehension and learning through comparing and contrasting languages.

I'm a Seed (Marzollo, 1996) is a beginning reader. It consists of a first person account of the plant life cycle.

Planting a Rainbow (Ehlert, 1988) consists of a child describing the ordering of flowering seeds and bulbs and then planting and caring for a flower garden. Its illustrations are labeled. A Spanish version (2006a) can improve comprehension and be used with the strategy compare and contrast.

Sunflower (Ford & Noll, 1995) is a short, simple, unrhymed poem. Its phrases describe the life cycle of the sunflower from a child's delighted point of view. It lends itself to the teaching strategy recitation.

STAGE 3: BOOKS WITH INCREASED COMPLEXITY

Stage 3 books contain an increased amount of linguistic complexity. They include new vocabulary, sentences types, and text structures while maintaining a reasonable amount of new language for ELLs to process. They contain devices found across academic texts, such as indexes and labeled illustrations. Again, a rule of thumb is that a Stage 3 book has about 70 words and their variants but about 20 new words to learn.

The book *It's Pumpkin Time!* (Hall & Halpern, 1994) is an example. It has two types of text. One is a patterned and culturally laden narrative about gardening and celebrating Halloween. The other is an end page with factual captions added to six illustrations of seed germination. The Spanish edition (2002) can be used for comprehension, comparison, and contrast.

Stage 3 books are within the range of ELLs who are able to process language of increasing complexity, such as manipulating sentences of five or more words. ELLs use these skills in substituting words to change meaning or to paraphrase without changing meaning. They can respond to the book in a wider variety of interactions than can readers of Stages 1 and 2 books, such as to give opinions, coherently summarize, answer questions with full sentences, and transfer between oral and written language. The following are more books categorized as Stage 3:

Carrot Soup (Segal, 2006) is a fictional story of a rabbit's gardening, which lays the groundwork for a tale of friendship. It lends itself to reader's theater and retelling strategies. In addition, the recipe on the end pages can be used with the LEA strategy.

The Grand Old Tree (DePalma, 2005) tells the sequential story of a complete life cycle. It contains poetic devices, such as metaphor and personification. Reenactment and recitation can be used to teach it.

How Does a Seed Grow? A Book With Foldout Pages (Kim, 2010) is an interactive science picture book with photographs and some technical vocabulary. Its question-and-answer format lends itself to the strategy guessing games.

A Seed Grows (Hickman & Collins, 1997b) has two types of text. One is a poetic and patterned running text, which lends itself to unison activities. The other is expository and uses academic devices, such as an index and an additional fact section under a flap. It can be used for comparing and contrasting different types of content as well as different genres of text.

STAGE 4: BOOKS WITH GREATER VARIETY FOR PRODUCTIVE BEGINNERS

Stage 4 books are longer and more complex than books in the first three stages. They often contain multiple types of texts, for example, a song accompanied by academic end notes. A rule of thumb is that a Stage 4 book contains no more than 500 words total, with up to 100 new words and their variants to be taught.

The book *The Dandelion Seed* (Anthony & Arbo, 1997) is an example. It is a poetic text about the seasons and cycle of life. It can be used to teach language arts content, such as personification. It can also be used with explicit vocabulary language-learning strategies.

Stage 4 books are within the range of productive beginners who are noticeably better than Stage 1–3 learners at processing new language in a familiar context. These ELLs can add and combine ideas from book-based activities into longer sentences and discourse (Kim, 2006). They are still considered beginners because they struggle in unfamiliar situations. Their conversations and writing about academic or unfamiliar topics contain frequent pauses and are slow because they grope for words. They need extra time to respond when they transfer visual information to verbal and oral to written. Four other examples of books for this stage include the following:

A Dandelion's Life (Himmelman, 1999) is a science picture book with expository text and accessible illustrations about a plant's life cycle. It can be taught with language teaching strategies that use graphic organizers. For example, using visual representations of text organization such as a Venn diagram for a text with comparisons and contrasts.

Mrs. Spitzer's Garden (Pattou, 2001) is about a garden but also is a character study of Mrs. Spitzer, the garden being a metaphor for her students. It can be taught with retelling.

Quiet in the Garden (Aliki, 2009) has two levels of text. The narrative is from a boy's point of view and includes observation, inquiry, and imagined responses. The back page gives gardening instructions. It lends itself to reader's theater and LEA.

One Bean (Rockwell, 1999) also has two styles of text. The story is a student's narration of the steps to planting. The end pages include bean-related activities usable with the LEA strategy.

OTHER HIGH-UTILITY PICTURE BOOKS ABOUT PLANTS

Several other useful books further round out the gardening theme. They provide opportunities to use formulaic language, encounter frequent phrases, and engage in language learning. *Clementina's Cactus* (Keats, 1999) is a wordless story with simple content. Wordless books are useful for differentiating for ELLs who need experience expressing themselves without written cues (Russell, 2000). I use *Clementina's Cactus* with retelling.

The running text of *Growing Vegetable Soup* (Ehlert, 2004a) is a Stage 2 sequential story. It also has other texts. It contains a soup recipe on the last page for use with the LEA strategy. Another set of useful texts are ones that contain scientific devices. *A Seed Is Sleepy* (Aston, 2007) includes scientific diagrams, a picture index, and labeled illustrations. *From Seed to Sunflower* (Legg & Scrace, 1998) is a realistic account of the life cycle of a sunflower and contains a table of contents, facts page, glossary, and index.

CONCLUSION

The first chapter described selecting picture books according to CLT principles, and the second chapter described selection according to content demands. This chapter focused on language difficulty. All three are used in searching for books for ELLs in different stages of beginner ELP. ELLs will participate in book-based interactions and learn faster when books are within their instructional range of English.

Organizing books by linguistic difficulty is complex because language itself is a complex construct made up of integrated and layered linguistic subsystems. A book's linguistic difficulty is the result of many linguistic variables; some are textual, but others result from the oral language used in delivering book-based instruction. A few key variables are enough to organize picture books into useful stages of beginner linguistic difficulty. They include evaluating text as to the number of new words, ratio of new words to total words, total number of running words, structural complexity, and its utility in a language learning context.

Beginner books are divided into four stages, each incrementally increasing the reader's linguistic processing load. Books with only a small amount of simple text are considered the first stage. Those with more text, but still simple, are a second, and those with more complexity are a third. Books with an increased number of words and amount of complexity are categorized into a fourth stage.

Of course, a number of great picture books for teaching ELLs do not fall into any of the four stages. They are often books that create contexts for sustained practice and interactive communication among students at different levels. These include wordless books, poetic texts, projects with directives, sequential fiction, and some informational formats. These high-utility texts remind us that aligning books to student linguistic abilities cannot be done in the abstract. It requires observing students' reactions and understanding of the book's written text and abilities to grasp and assimilate the language used in book-based activities. In Chapter 4, assessments for observing students are presented.

TELLABILITY IN PRACTICE: DETERMINING LANGUAGE DIFFICULTY FOR BEGINNER ELLS

Select one of the books from the list in Box 3.2 and evaluate it according to the concepts discussed in the chapter. Repeat this with a book from your classroom or library.

Consider key linguistic variables for determining difficulty for beginner ELLs in answering the following questions:

3.1. What is the amount of language in the text?

3.2. What is level of language complexity?

3.3. How much of each is present in the book?

Box 3.2	Examples of Books Organized by Incremental Language Difficulty	
Categories	*ELL Behaviors*	*Sample Books*
Stage 1	Recognizes words in familiar contexts. Uses the simplest verbal expression and nonlinguistic means of answering questions.	*Green Starts: In the Garden* (IKids, 2009) *My Garden/Mi Jardin* (Emberley, 2008) *Pumpkin, Pumpkin* (Titherington, 1986) *Ten Seeds* (Brown, 2001b) *Diez Semillas* (2001a) *Up, Down, and Around* (Ayres, 2007)
Stage 2	Understands nouns, verbs, and concrete language in patterned sentences and structures. Uses common words and answers questions haltingly in one- to two-word phrases and formulas.	*The Carrot Seed* (Kraus, 1988) *La Semilla de Zanahoria* (Kraus, 1996) *Flower Garden* (Bunting, 2000) or *Flower Garden/ Jardin de Flores* (Bunting, 1994) *I'm a Seed* (Marzollo, 1996) *Planting a Rainbow* (Ehlert, 1988) *Sunflower* (Ford & Noll, 1995)
Stage 3	Understands linguistic patterns across subsystems. Uses a variety of words and sentences of five or more words. Answers questions with full sentences.	*Carrot Soup* (Segal, 2006) *The Grand Old Tree* (DePalma, 2005) *How Does a Seed Grow? A Book With Foldout Pages* (Kim, 2010) *It's Pumpkin Time!* (Hall & Halpern, 1994) *¡Tiempo de Calabazas!* (Hall & Halpern, 2002) *A Seed Grows* (Hickman & Collins, 1997b)

(Continued)

(Continued)

Categories	ELL Behaviors	Sample Books
Stage 4	Understands and coherently retells stories and factual information. Uses language to expand, combine, add details, and transfer information.	*A Dandelion's Life* (Himmelman, 1999) *The Dandelion Seed* (Anthony & Arbo, 1997) *Mrs. Spitzer's Garden* (Pattou, 2001) *One Bean* (Rockwell, 1999) *Quiet in the Garden* (Aliki, 2009)
High Utility	Engages in open-ended language learning and book-based tasks.	*Clementina's Cactus* (Keats, 1999) wordless. *From Seed to Sunflower (Lifecycles)* (Legg & Scrace, 1998) *Growing Vegetable Soup* (Ehlert, 2004a) *Jack's Garden* (Cole, 1995) *A Seed Is Sleepy* (Aston, 2007)

4

Assessments for Matching Books and English Language Learners

In an ideal world, it would be easy to find the right picture book for all beginner English language learners (ELLs), one with just the right level of content, language, and format to provide a maximum amount of support for their second-language learning. In the real world, it is not always easy to find them. Finding picture books within ELLs' instructional range requires attention to the book's content, language, and format. It also requires paying close attention to the students' abilities as they engage in book-based language learning.

To do this, I use Wiggins and McTighe's (2005) notion of finding out what the students already understand, can do, and need. In the communicative language teaching (CLT) context, it involves observing their oral and written skills across the communicative competencies. Assessment tools can facilitate observing student's abilities to listen, speak, read, and write in response to picture books. The best tools provide seamless transfer to instruction. As Boyd-Batstone explains, "The teacher needs a quick assessment of proficiency levels based upon characteristic behaviors for each level and a ready reference for which strategies and activities would be appropriate for instruction" (2006, p. 7).

Fortunately, there are many resources with quick assessments of beginning oral and written skills (Boyd-Batstone, 2006; Curtain &

Dahlberg, 2010; Gottlieb, 2006; Opitz & Guccione, 2009; Uribe & Nathenson-Mejía, 2008). The best assessment tools adhere to principles of language testing; for example, a test should require only the amount of time needed to collect the necessary information to make an instructional decision. Tests should be proportionate to improving teaching effectiveness and efficiency.

Let me introduce assessment tools to use with beginner picture books by way of a vignette. The scene is my first visit to a summer program for beginner ELLs in fifth through seventh grades. Most of the books used as examples here are on the transportation theme. The list of books at the end of the chapter includes additional titles for a wider range of grades.

VIGNETTE: A FOUR-BY-FOUR MATRIX

Before my first day of teaching ELLs in pullout lessons, their classroom teacher provided me with brief descriptions of each student's proficiency. Her bulleted summaries used commonly accepted terms for describing English language proficiency (ELP). The four bulleted summaries below are samples that illustrate these descriptions. (Random capital letters are used in place of student names.)

- A, silent. -> 1) Needs oral language and basic vocabulary.[1] Talk! Goes everywhere with a classroom buddy. 2) Copies legibly with neat printing. She arrived two months ago. Writes Vietnamese.
- D, silent. -> 1) Needs to talk (very shy), vocabulary, writing. 2) Writes with help but avoids it. Spanish.
- B, emerging in speech. -> 1) Talks a lot. Needs grammatically correct models for oral—confuses verb tenses (past/present/future). 2) Writing needs help with sentence structure. Sends daily e-mails to her friend in Korea.
- C, high beginner -> 1) Actively listens in conversations and talks a lot on topics he chooses. 2) Needs writing—mixes Spanish in.

These notes provided key information on oral and written language abilities. I transferred it onto a four-by-four matrix. I used the matrix to select teaching strategies and leveled books, to group students, and to plan my first lessons.

Box 4.1   Four-by-Four Matrix

Name:	Stage One Silent	Stage Two Early Emergent	Stage Three Emergent	Stage Four Productive Beginner
Listening	D A		B	C
Speaking	D A		B	C
Reading	A	D	B C	
Writing	A	D	B C	

The four-by-four matrix provided me with data to confidently select books at the right level of instructional challenge and to maximize instructional time. I began the first day by having small leveled groups of ELLs examine a few books within their ELP range. Each ELL was allowed to select one book from the assortment. Giving students choices is an essential principle in CLT.

Students A and D were experiencing their first encounters with English; therefore, the books were short and simple and had transparent illustrations. The topics included only cars and bicycles, and the books had basic words and short sentences; they included *My Car* (Barton, 2001), *This Car* (Collicutt, 2002) and *Bicycle Race* (Crews, 1985). The students found them easy to comprehend. They developed confidence and fluency in English expression with each rereading, retelling, and rewriting. They used them to study the English used during interactions with books in general, such as learning to count page numbers, use directives, and answer questions using *yes/no* and *which one.* They also studied the text through word sorting and substitution.

The books I selected for students B and C were further along on the beginner difficulty continuum. I expanded the content to airplanes and boats because these students already knew enough language about numbers, the alphabet, cars, and bicycles. They were faster at processing English, and, therefore, the books I selected were longer. The inclusion of a greater range of topics resulted in a noticeable increase in vocabulary, such as verbs and locations. They learned to ask and answer questions with *what, who, where,* and *when.* We began with *This Plane* (Collicutt, 2000), *This Boat* (Collicutt, 2001), *Sail Away* (Crews, 1995a), and *Who Sank the Boat?* (Allen, 1996). Just as with the earlier group, the activities emphasized comprehension, expression, language learning, and fluency.

During subsequent lessons, I tracked students' progress using informal assessment tools providing information on their listening, speaking, reading, and writing. The assessments allowed me to note each student's progress in each skill, reform the groups, and plan accordingly.

The types of assessments I used are the following:

1. Listening with a total physical response (TPR) rubric and a comprehension check

2. Speaking with a retelling scale

3. Reading with an I-We-U interview and a graphic organizer

4. Writing with a writing scale and timed writing

These tools are used to record observations of each student and compare them against benchmarks within the beginner ELP level. They can be supplemented with additional teacher-developed tests based on the specific language taught in a book-based lesson. It is also helpful to record anecdotal information about students, such as their ability to transfer between oral and written skills.

LISTENING: TPR RUBRIC

TPR is a popular CLT strategy for teaching comprehension to beginners. The strategy requires ELLs to listen to a command and respond accordingly. During picture book activities, teachers demonstrate physically the meaning of verbs. Students imitate them. As the students become familiar with them, the teacher gradually decreases her or his cues.

This strategy does not rely on written text. However, written prompts can be used. Picture books with action verbs lend themselves to using this strategy. ELLs learn the verbs in the text and those used in the context of reading it in class. For example, using the book, *Send It!* (Carter, 2003), a story about sending a package, ELLs learn the verbs in the story, such as *carry, stack, drop, address,* and *wrap;* and verbs used in oral language surrounding language learning activities, such as *point to the address, turn the page,* and *hold the book up.* TPR is invaluable in teaching beginners comprehension, and it lends itself to monitoring student development of this essential language skill.

Comprehension can be measured with a TPR rubric. The example included here is an adaptation of the TPR rubric developed by Paul Boyd-Batstone (2006). It is used to record ELLs' receptive language behaviors. The left column of the rubric contains criteria statements organized by gradually increasing difficulty. The other columns allow recording of incremental progress, for example, to distinguish between silent beginners who comprehend and students who do not comprehend. Silent beginners who do not understand would have a check in the second column under the heading *None.* Silent beginners who do understand would have a check in the third or fourth column. The rubric also includes a way to record whether ELLs comprehend directives given orally or in writing.

TPR Rubric Procedure

1. Make note of the routine requests you will use in the fifth column, such as *point to* and *your turn.*

2. Make a list of the action verbs (TPR commands) from the book.

3. Select criteria (the number of directives and commands required) for the third and fourth columns, *Few* and *Most.* For example, *few* might be one to five correct responses out of ten opportunities to respond, and *most* might be six or more.

4. Conduct TPR activities, and record each student's abilities on the form. The letter *o* can be used to note when the directive is oral and *w* when it is written.

Example: TPR Rubric Assessment

Criteria	None	Few 1–5/10	Most 6–10/10	Comments / Sample List of Directives
Stage 1. One-step oral commands. Written commands.				point to, pick up, your turn, hand me the book, turn the page
Stage 2. Oral commands involving verbs, nouns. Written commands.				
Stage 3. Oral commands involving verbs, nouns, and adjectives such as color, number, and shape. Written commands.				
Stage 4. Two-step oral commands. Written commands.				

Source: Adapted from Boyd-Batstone, 2006.

LISTENING: COMPREHENSION CHECK

Another way to observe students' listening comprehension behaviors is to design a comprehension check. This is administered much like a spelling test, but the teacher makes a listening comprehension check form using illustrations of a book's content words. The students mark them according to the teacher's directions. For example, they are to find illustrations of key vocabulary words and mark them as directed. For the comprehension check of the book *Send It!* I used these items:

1. Underline the package.

2. Circle the mail truck.

3. Put an x on the address.

An example of a comprehension check is included in the TPR lesson plan for the book *Mama Cat has Three Kittens* (Flemming, 1998) in the appendix.

The TPR rubric and comprehension check are examples of assessments for listening comprehension that a whole class can work on at once. However, in CLT there are times when conferencing with individual students is required. The following reading comprehension assessment can be used with individuals.

READING: I-WE-U INTERVIEW RECORD

The I-We-U interview is a gradual-release CLT strategy, in which the teacher models the reading of a story several times. With each rereading, more of the responsibility for reading is given over to the student. For example, in the first reading, the student follows along. After a second reading, the student helps the teacher read. In a third reading, the student reads while the teacher guides, prompts, praises, and allows the student to take on more of the reading task. In the final reading, the student reads independently. Throughout the process, teachers interview students and engage them by commenting, encouraging questions, discussing ideas, and making connections between oral and written language.

The I-We-U interview guides ELLs to develop comprehension and fluency as well as oral reading accuracy. Teachers must prepare literal, inferential, and opinion questions and record these on the I-We-U interview sheet, so that the same questions are asked with each administration. This makes it easy to compare the ELL's responses over time.

Sample Assessments for the I-We-U Record

The following are sample assessments associated with beginner ELP stages using the books *Bicycle Race* (Crews, 1985) and *Sail Away* (Crews, 1995a):

Stage 1 questions based on reading *Bicycle Race*

Can the students show comprehension of 10 *yes/no* questions by pointing, drawing, or acting? For example, do they comprehend the questions, "Is number nine first?" or "Did number nine win?"

Do their responses to *which one* questions make sense? For example, do they understand "Which one is broken?" or "Which rider is first?"

Stage 2 questions based on reading *Bicycle Race*

What factual questions do the students answer orally and in writing? For example, can they answer, "What is the title?" or "Where are the crowds?"

Do they express themselves using the English words found in the text? For example, can they say, "Where is number nine?" or "Who was last?"

Stage 3 questions based on reading *Sail Away*

What inferential questions do students answer? For example, can they answer, "Is the boat sailing down river?" or "Do you think it's sailing fast?"

Do they express more than literal facts found in the text? For example, do they ask "What did the sailors feel?" or "Did you like this story?"

Stage 4 questions based on reading *Sail Away*

What do students expand or expound upon? For example, do they ask, "What would you do?"

Do they generalize the new text language to other contexts? For example, do they ask, "What is similar in this story to other stories?"

Observe ELL responses, and record these on the I-We-U interview record. Later, review these records to reflect on what they know, understand, and need to know. These observations are useful for planning subsequent lessons.

READING: GRAPHIC ORGANIZER

Another way to observe reading comprehension of ELLs engaged in lessons with picture books is to teach them to take notes on graphic organizers, such as a concept map or story map. A sample story map is included in the retelling lesson plan included in the appendix. Graphic organizers allow them to show understanding regardless of their ELP level. ELLs can create a visual display of content and relationships between concepts.

The task of showing comprehension with a graphic can be as simple as copying information onto an already developed graphic or as sophisticated as creating one. In using them as assessment tools, the teacher scores the ELL's graphic according to the objective of the learning task. For example, when the ELLs are required to fill in the graphic organizer with key words from the text, the teacher might require a certain number of words to be included. This can show the students' grasp of information. Alternatively, the teacher might require them to select an appropriate graphic for a text. This can show their ability to represent relationships among concepts. As ELLs' comprehension increases, their graphic organizers include more detailed and comprehensive information.

Story maps are visual representations of the essential elements of a story. They are useful in guiding ELLs in integrated oral and written language tasks. Beginner ELLs can use story maps as a resource for processing the story elements. For example, after filling in a story map based on *Who Sank the Boat?* (Allen, 1996), sixth graders used their maps as templates for planning similar personalized versions of the story. For one ELL, the map provided the basis for a funny recollection of being at the pool titled *Who Sank My Raft? My Little Sister*.

Graphic organizers scaffold reading comprehension and help ELLs develop skills in transferring back and forth between graphic and text representations of concepts. They also help ELLs to integrate written and oral language skills as they scaffold listening, retelling, summarizing, and rewriting. Graphic organizers can be used as an assessment tool by devising a scoring system, for example counting the number of facts a student records after listening to a book. In a sense, they provide evidence of listening and written expression. The next assessment tool focuses on recording oral expression.

SPEAKING: A RETELLING SCALE

Retelling is an essential skill, and it is ubiquitous in CLT. The retelling scale is one tool to use to record ELLs' developing abilities to produce meaningful oral English. It is a record of spontaneous retelling of stories as well as thoughtfully prepared book talks. The scale shown below is designed to record beginning expressive abilities, which rely heavily on context, prompts, visuals, and text. It includes benchmark statements of ability and can be adapted to reflect different CLT strategies and the use of different prompts.

While text is a wonderful resource and scaffolds oral expression, there are ELLs who use it as a crutch. These students need opportunities to develop and practice oral exchanges without using text (Weber, 2009). Wordless picture books can be used in teaching and testing speaking skills. Teachers can identify ways ELLs can improve their intelligibility. ELLs can focus on a particularly difficult pattern or the use of paralanguage, such as intonation, pitch, tempo, tone, gestures, and facial expression. Wordless books on the topic of transportation include *Plane* (Felix, 1994), *Ships Ahoy* (Sis, 1999), *Truck* (Crews, 1991) and *Ed Emberley's Drawing Book: Make a World* (Emberley, 2006c). A teacher should preplan the language used with the books to ensure the language sample is within the ELLs' capacity.

Retelling Scale Procedure

1. Select a book and the key vocabulary to frontload.[2]

2. Share the book with a picture walk[3] and shared reading aloud.

3. Prepare a scoring sheet, such as the one shown below. Write the prompts in the left column on the form.

4. Give each ELL time to engage in reviewing the book, or in the case of a prepared book talk, time to rehearse.

5. Ask each ELL to retell the story. Take notes as to your use of prompts.

6. For a prepared book talk,[4] rehearse over several days, and have ELLs work on pronunciation goals for specific pages.

7. Record the book talk scores, and plan subsequent lessons accordingly.

Scoring with the following retelling scale is based on noting stages within the beginner level. It begins with Stage 1, those who cannot retell basic information but may express themselves by non-English means, such as gestures or in their native language. Stage 2 is for those who retell limited information using text-bound vocabulary. Stage 3 ELLs' expression reflects the text and the use of text as a resource. Finally, Stage 4 beginners can retell from memory.

Retelling Scale

Date: Prompts:	Name: _____ Book Title: _____
	Spontaneous Retelling _____ Prepared Book Talk _____
	Reader's Theater _____ Recital _____ Other _____
	Stage 1—Difficulty with task. Unintelligible.
	_____ Non-English retelling.
	_____ Expresses meaning using illustrations, drawing, gestures, or minimal words.
	Comments/objective: _____
	Stage 2—Text-bound recall.
	_____ Expression is text-bound and contingent on illustrations.
	_____ Retells key names, items, and actions. Vocabulary used in simple sentences.
	Comments/objective: _____
	Stage 3—Text-based recall.
	_____ Expression refers to text and illustrations.
	_____ Retells key details with organizational devices.

(Continued)

(Continued)

Comments/objective: _____

Stage 4—Text is catalyst for expression.

_____ Information presented at normal speed.

_____ Retells intelligibly with more than one of the following: introduction, story elements, summary, conclusion, response to audience.

Comments/objective: _____

Reflections/plans: _____

The retelling scale can be adapted for use in observing expressive ability when students engage in dramatic performances, such as musicals, reader's theater, or poetry recitals. Before the performance, make a list of things to look for as each student performs. For example, students can be required to practice specific interpretive devices or the use of paralanguage, such as a particular intonation, pitch, tempo, gesture, or facial expression. These can be included in the scale. For example, in an oral presentation of Shulevitz's *Dawn* (1988), students can be told to pause and whisper to emphasize the quietness of the lake, to tap their fingers as they say that the oars rattled, and add appropriate gestures when speaking about the call of a bird. Another example of student requirements might be to have the ELLs agree upon a minimum number of meaningful gestures to make, such as one per line while performing the song in *The Wheels on the Bus* (Raffi, 1990).

Finally, assessments can be developed to record oral skills being taught through integrated tasks. The language experience approach (LEA) lesson included in the appendix is an example of integrated teaching of oral and written skills with picture books containing projects. Two books lending themselves to integrated teaching and testing on the transportation theme are *Ed Emberley's Drawing Book: Make a World* (Emberley, 2006c) and *Crafts for Kids Who Are Learning About Transportation* (Ross, 2006).

WRITING SCALES

Beginner ELLs come to the task of learning to write English with a wide variety of literacy levels and backgrounds. For this reason, our assessments of writing must address a wide range of written skills. Writing scales, an authentic assessment of written language, are useful for collecting information about the abilities of ELLs. Writing scales allow teachers to compare a student's writing to a broad-based record of leveled written samples or descriptions.

The content of a writing scale reflects the focus of instruction. The writing scale provided here lends itself to picture book contexts. It assumes picture books are being used as templates and scaffolds in model-based writing instruction. The use of dialogue journals is one of the most popular manifestations of model-based writing with ELLs.

Using dialogue journals is a strategy in which students and teacher write personalized letters to each other. While dialogue journals are about contextualized topics, with ELLs they are used to develop language rather than content (Peregoy & Boyle, 2005). Teachers' written responses to students' writing promote ELP development through modeling. Teachers instruct by asking written questions requiring students to notice ways in which their writing is misunderstood. Dialogue journals are an excellent resource for monitoring language ability over time. The following writing scale sample assumes ELLs are writing dialogue journals about picture book–based lessons.

Procedure for Using Writing Scales

1. Prepare the writing scale form, writing prompts, and model answers. The sample scale below includes beginner writing behaviors categorized into four developmental stages. The second column can be used for book-specific examples.

2. Select and share a book of interest to the ELLs. Here are some suggested questions to use in engaging them in responding:
   - What is it about? It is about ____.
   - What does it remind you of? It reminds me of ____.
   - Which part do you like? I liked ____.
   - What was your favorite part? My favorite part was ____.
   - What did you love about it? I loved ____.
   - Who was ____? ____ was ____.
   - What did you find interesting? ____ is interesting.

3. After sharing the book with the ELLs, ask them to write about it in their dialogue journals. Provide them with specific instructions as to the number of sentences they are to write, the amount of time allotted, and expected outcomes.

4. Compare their writing at two different points in time; the scale below has two columns for different dates.

Writing Scales

Name:	Picture book used: _____ Assignment: Is the ELL literate in native language? Y/N	Date:	Date:
Stage 1	1. Copies manuscript alphabet, name, address, and titles. 2. Writes name, school name, labels, numbers, and number words, such as *first, second,* et cetera. 3. Labels from memory. Answers choice questions such as *which one __?* 4. Takes dictation of vocabulary from memory.		
Stage 2	1. Copies legibly. 2. Writes bits of information in phrases, labels pictures, writes affirmative statements from memory. 3. Writes new information, new simple sentences, and answers to *yes/no* questions. 4. Takes dictation of statements in negative and plural forms.		
Stage 3	1. Uses transitional spelling and phonic cues. 2. Transfers vocabulary across contexts. 3. Uses prewriting strategies and questions to write. Transfers between WH (who? what? where? why? which? when? how?) questions and answers. 4. Transfers and inflects for person and tense.		
Stage 4	1. Writes script using conventional spelling. 2. Applies academic signal words and phrases—such as *first, then, finally,* and *compare to*—in short paragraphs, and uses information questions in complete sentences. 3. Uses literary devices reflecting genre or text structure. 4. Transfers information from books, graphs, and graphic organizers to narrative or expository paragraphs.		

TIMED WRITING

Another common CLT writing assessment is a timed writing. Its focus is fluency. It simply involves the following steps:

1. ELLs write the book's title on the top of a sheet of paper as well as the date and amount of allotted time in minutes.

2. At the beginning of the allotted time, they write as accurately and as much as they can about the book.

3. Once the time is up, they count the total number of words and calculate the words per minute (WPM).

4. WPM can be calculated and recorded every couple of weeks and compared over time.

The sample assessments included here address language skills ELLs learn when engaged with picture books. Each should be adapted to meet the verbal, visual, and experiential features of the books and the instructional context.

They also must be flexibly adjusted to the parameters of each instructional context. For example, while the TPR rubric targets listening comprehension, it can also be modified to accommodate the use of written commands, and in this way it incorporates assessment of the ELL's ability to recognize written words. So too, the retelling scale targets spoken expression, but it can be modified to check progress in writing by evaluating the ELLs' written plans for a book talk.

CONCLUSION

Assessing ELLs' language usage during book-based lessons is critical for lesson planning. They must address the four skills of listening, reading, speaking, and writing. These skills are learned as part of a balanced program of CLT, during comprehension, expression, language-focused learning, and fluency instruction. We use the information collected to determine what our students know, can do, and need, so we can select books and teaching strategies appropriately.

The next and last chapter completes the process of finding books with tellability. Its focus is on finding books with specific features associated with language teaching strategies. Synergy between a book and a CLT strategy creates efficiencies for teachers and students. The chapter describes the types of books to use with 12 particular CLT strategies.

TELLABILITY IN PRACTICE: ASSESSMENT OF SKILLS

Select one of the assessments of the chapter and adapt it for use with a particular book and group of ELLs.

4.1 What would this assessment tell you about the ELLs' knowledge, skills, and abilities in oral or written English?

4.2 What would you plan for students who score poorly, well, or excellently on this assessment?

Box 4.2 Books About Transportation[5]	
Stages	*Suggested Books*
Stage 1. Focus on comprehension.	*All Aboard! A Traveling Alphabet* (Demarest & Mayer, 2008) has the alphabet. *Bicycle Race* (Crews, 1985) teaches number words. *Flying* (Crews, 1986) has thematic vocabulary. *School Bus* (Crews, 1993) has thematic vocabulary. *Send it!* (Carter, 2003) has the days of week. Appeals to younger ELLs. *That's Not My Plane* (Watt, 2008) has patterned sentences. Appropriate for lower grade ELLs.
Stage 2. Focus on expression.	*Airplanes* (Barton, 1998) has thematic vocabulary and simple illustrations. *Amelia's Fantastic Flight* (Bursik, 1994) has poetic devices. *My Car* (Barton, 2001) has a sequential story. Barton's simple illustrations appeal to lower grade ELLs. *This Car* (Collicutt, 2002) has sentence patterns. *This Plane* (Collicutt, 2001) has sentence patterns. *What Do Wheels Do All Day?* (Prince, 2006) is a rhyming concept book.
Stage 3. Focus on explicit learning of patterns.	*Airport* (Barton, 1982) has thematic vocabulary and simple illustrations. *Dawn* (Shulevitz, 1988) has a sequential story. *Harbor* (Crews, 1987) has thematic vocabulary. *I Love Planes!* (Sturges & Halpern, 2003) has poetic devices. The main character is in a lower grade. *Sail Away* (Crews, 1995a) has a sequential story. *This Boat* (Collicutt, 2001) has sentence patterns.

Stages	Suggested Books
Stage 4. Focus on fluent production.	*Angela's Airplane* (Munsch, 1988) is a young girl's adventure story. *Airplanes! Soaring! Diving! Turning!* (Hubbell, Halsey, & Addy, 2008) uses descriptive rhyming text with graphics. *Cars! Rushing! Honking! Zooming!* (Hubbell, 2010) has theme vocabulary. *Crafts for Kids Who Are Learning About Transportation* (Ross, 2006) has directions for projects. *The Wheels on the Bus* (Raffi, 1990) contains lyrics. *Who Sank the Boat?* (Allen, 1996) has a story structure.

Box 4.3   Wordless Books Cited

Ed Emberley's Drawing Book: Make a World (Emberley, 2006c).

Plane (Felix, 1994).

Ships Ahoy (Sis, 1999). Main character is young.

Truck (Crews, 1991).

NOTES

1. In teaching ELLs, basic vocabulary refers to the 1,000 most useful words for everyday transactions, here-and-now contexts, high-frequency actions, concrete nouns, and palpable modifiers. These are found on the General Service List (GSL).

2. Frontloading occurs when a teacher prepares students for a text with explicit instruction of the critical vocabulary. It builds the linguistic background needed to understand a text prior to instruction.

3. A picture walk occurs when a teacher prepares students for a picture book by browsing through the pictures in order. It builds the students' ability to interpret the story by drawing on their background experiences and analysis of the illustrations.

4. A book talk is a teaching strategy in which students discuss a book they have read or heard with classmates.

5. With few exceptions, these books are appropriate for upper grade ELLs. The exceptions are noted.

5 Matching Books to Communicative Language Teaching Strategies

As every teacher knows, learning flows when there is synchronicity among students, teaching strategies, and instructional materials. Communicative language teaching (CLT) strategies can be selected to capitalize on picture book features to achieve this flow. Harmony between picture books and teaching strategies lessens the linguistic load required for book-based activities. It creates more opportunities to reinforce, solidify, and practice new language and thus accelerates language learning. In Chapter 1, the Dr. Seuss Day vignette described the flow created by using *From Head to Toe* (Carle, 2003). This book facilitated student participation in three CLT strategies. The 12 active verbs complemented a CLT strategy requiring gestures, total physical response (TPR). The repetitive question was ideal for a unison CLT strategy, chanting, and the patterned sentences lent themselves to teaching with substitution.

The same lesson with a different book would not provide the same easy connections and would have required teacher-developed adjustments. For example, the book *Brown Bear, Brown Bear, What Do You See?*

(Martin & Carle, 1992) is compatible with chanting and with substitution but not TPR. In order to use this book with TPR, a teacher would have to add active verbs to a book-based activity. This is not difficult to do, because this book contains animals that can be dramatized. Making a list of animal movements is relatively easy. For example, English language learners (ELLs) can learn *fly, pounce,* and *waddle* and be asked to *fly like a bird, pounce like a cat,* and *waddle like a duck.* My point is that this requires the teacher to expend extra time and effort to prepare lists and make cue cards.

It is common practice in beginning reading pedagogy to match books to teaching strategies. In fact, a good many book lists are annotated and organized around instructional strategies. For example, it is easy to find lists of books that have "repetitive and patterned" text. This type of text is used for implementing the shared reading strategy. This makes sense in teaching emergent readers who know English. The teacher guides them in unison reading and reciting. For the average English-speaking student, patterned and repetitious texts are equally difficult. The differences are not enough to list them separately on a list of good books for shared reading.

For beginning ELLs, this is not the case. Many ELLs can successfully engage in a repetitious task before being able to engage in learning with patterned texts. Thus for ELLs, these two text variables are important. Describing a book's tellability requires a more nuanced description that details whether the text is repetitious, patterned, or both. Knowing this is important for matching a book to students. It is also important in selecting a CLT strategy. We do not want to gloss over the nuanced distinctions, because instructional flow is achieved differently with repetitive texts than it is with patterned texts.

Patterned sentences introduce more new vocabulary than repetitive ones. Patterns are used for vocabulary expansion with ELLs. They teach ELLs about meanings conveyed through word class[1] categories and sentence structures. Patterned sentences in CLT are often used in substitution tasks. ELLs must know an appropriate set of words in order to be able to replace words as they make new sentences following the pattern. For example, in one activity they learn to replace the given subject noun with another noun. In another, they will be substituting a verb phrase with others.

Repetitious texts are used quite differently in CLT. Repetitive texts are ideal for teaching fluency. Repetition is one of the key fluency strategies that focus on improving speed and accuracy because the text and vocabulary are known.

Essential components of CLT differ from those of teaching reading, and the annotations of book lists should reflect these differences. One of the major differences is the development of oral expressive and receptive skills along with written ones. Many CLT strategies focus on oral development. Thus, it is useful to describe a book as having features matching oral strategies. Having books annotated as compatible to a CLT strategy will automatically be enough information to create synchronicity for a second-language instructional situation.

RATIONALE FOR 12 CLT STRATEGIES

The descriptions of books in the tellability list in the appendix use 12 CLT strategies. The rationale for using 12 CLT strategies is practical. It makes for a manageable organization of thematic book-based lessons adhering to parameters of a balanced CLT program. The 12 strategies meet the following criteria: Together they

1. create opportunities to develop oral and written language comprehension, expression, study, and fluency;

2. match features found in individual picture books (books can be found that contain enough noticeable examples);

3. match features found in a number of picture books (there are more than a dozen sparse-text picture books with this feature); and

4. appear in books with topics relevant and appealing to school-aged ELLs.

The rationale is summed up in one overriding principle: "Less is more." When strategies and books match, beginners can focus on deeply processing an instructionally manageable amount of language. Having books annotated with a compatible CLT strategy helps us better select books for the purpose of accelerating the development of new language skills.

As was described in the earlier example of patterned versus repetitious text, CLT requires paying attention to essential elements for second-language learning as opposed to teaching English speakers to read. Thus, these CLT strategies reflect a beginner's need to focus attention on developing oral language, basic vocabulary, and fluency. The following section explores some of these essential language elements. After it, each of the 12 CLT strategies is described along with examples of compatible books about tiny animals.

ORAL AND WRITTEN LANGUAGE STYLES

We know from Cummins's work (1981, 1991), briefly described in Chapter 2, that ELLs confronted with learning language and content together benefit from added contextual support and familiar concepts. As was pointed out, a text with limited cognitive demands allows second-language learners to focus on developing English language proficiency (ELP). The dual demands of content and language are not the only barriers for beginners. Many texts make dual demands because the written text is quite different from the typical oral language used by beginners.

When planning instruction for ELLs, teachers must take into account the differences between written and oral language (Rost, 2006). Written language is considered to be inherently more difficult than oral language. Academically oriented texts are particularly difficult for beginners. Certain features of academic text are beyond their level of comprehension. For example, academic texts often contain syntactic complexity, lexical density, a paucity of contextual references, unfamiliar or infrequently used vocabulary, and ideas presented in an integrated succession (Rost, 2006). For beginners, written texts pose significant barriers.

In contrast, oral language is often considered to be much easier than written language. It is usually supported by a here-and-now referent, such as the pictures of a book (Rost, 2006). Rost (2006) describes the oral language features thought to make it easy to teach ELLs. Compared to written language, it has a single referent per verb phrase, is presented with social cues, has limited and repetitive vocabulary, uses declarative forms, and repeats personal pronouns. However, oral language is really not much easier than written; it is just different and experienced with contextual supports.

Learning oral English is not simple and beginners find its complexity overwhelming. This issue is relevant to matching CLT strategies to picture books (Chafe & Danielewicz, 1987). Understanding it helps us to achieve synchronicity between ELLs, teaching strategies, and books, and this is essential to selecting books with tellability. Several aspects of the issue will be discussed below.

First, oral language spoken at normal speed is too complex for beginners to comprehend (August & Shanahan, 2006; Opitz & Guccione, 2009; Rost, 2006). Its fleeting and illusive nature makes deciphering basic linguistic units, patterns, and communicative devices difficult. Beginners must devote effort and concentrated attention to processing words, sentences, and discourse. While they focus on one subsystem or competency, they miss important clues in others.

Second, teachers are often encouraged to present oral language explanations when presenting written language. While for English speakers this mediation is a scaffold, using oral language complicates input for ELLs. They must simultaneously decipher new oral and written language forms. For beginning ELLs, it can sometimes feel like learning two languages. Oral styles often contain words that are infrequently used in written text. For a beginner, an oral explanation can be so different from the text that it confuses rather than helps. The ELLs find it difficult to learn oral forms, new oral vocabulary, new written vocabulary, and, at the same time, the skill of transferring back and forth between the two. They need extra processing time and limited amounts of text. This is why, in CLT, it is standard practice to allow second-language learners to read passages silently before being asked to read aloud (Gunderson, 2009); otherwise, comprehension suffers.

The dual challenge of learning oral and written language is reflected in beginner-level second-language materials. Beginner texts often reflect the author's desire to reduce the linguistic load. Some start with only oral samples, and others start with a focus on written language samples. Beginner-level materials might be composed of written text that mimics oral dialogue or written style text for oral practice. While these texts also appear inauthentic, they are often effective and valid stepping-stones until more authentic materials can be used effectively.

Tellability is an effective response to the dilemma of the dual challenge of oral and written language. Carefully selected picture books work because they are authentic examples of native speaker language. By using books with manageable amounts of new language, instructional flow is improved. This is because we can take advantage of congruities between the oral language of a CLT strategy and the written language in the book. The following questions help to select books with tellability:

1. What feature is noticeably compatible with a particular CLT strategy?

2. Does the book also include compatibilities with additional CLT strategies?

3. How many incidences of the features are in the book?

These strategies are also listed in the preface. In the following section, a brief description of each strategy, as well as examples of books about bugs and tiny animals, is provided. The chapter concludes with the list of books cited.

CHANTING AND SINGING

Chanting and singing are oral unison activities commonly used in CLT. They do not need written text, since the purpose is to develop pronunciation, intonation, and rhythm. Chanting, made popular with the publication of *Jazz Chants* by Carolyn Graham in 1978, was developed for conversational fluency. Betty Smallwood's publication of a list of singable books boosted the use of songs (Smallwood & Haynes, 2008).

The reason for using unison oral language tasks with beginners is to reduce anxiety. Beginners experience frequent breakdowns, which are frustrating, so they often avoid engaging in communicative interactions (Chamot & O'Malley, 1994; Hamayan, 1994). The repetition inherent in these strategies provides predictability, leading to success. It gives beginners opportunities to participate and build fluency by copying, approximating, and imitating (Holdaway, 1982; Rasinski & Padak, 2001). ELLs memorize sentences, and this familiarity makes substitution and cloze possible.

> The cloze sentence can be written on a sentence strip, with individual students asked to use their word banks to find words that will fit into the deleted slot. . . . Set cloze sentences can be written to include particular classes of words so that students get practice with them. (Gunderson, 2009, p. 131)

The best books for chanting are short enough to be reread and/or have repetition of phrases and sentences. Books with lyrics and musical scores are compatible with singing. An especially fun book in the list below is the folk song "The Ants Came Marching." Students can also sing it while reenacting or marching out the door to the playground.

Books for Chanting and Singing Listed Alphabetically

The Ants Came Marching (Kelly, 2000) is a folk song illustrated for all age groups.

Beetle Bop (Fleming, 2007) has patterned couplets for chanting.

Hey, Little Ant (Hoose & Hoose, 1998) contains the lyrics to a song.

Spider on the Floor (Raffi, 1996) comes with a CD.

COMPARE AND CONTRAST

Strategies using contrasting and comparing of two languages were originally developed by Charles Fries (1945) and in 1957 were expanded and clarified by Robert Lado. Today, comparing and contrasting tasks are popular for teaching a broad range of communicative competencies (August & Shanahan, 2006; Calderon, 2004; Chamot, 2005; Oxford; 2006; Petitto, 2003). They accelerate language achievement when applied as an intentional language learning strategy.

The key to effective use of the compare and contrast strategy is to adjust its implementation to the nature of the content, the language features of the text, and the language learning needs of the ELLs. Books with parallel concepts are a natural for using this strategy. For example, books with objects lend themselves to teaching comparatives and superlatives, with repeated information in different genres to teach literary devices, and bilingual books to analyze distinctions between the ELLs' native language and English.

The utility of using bilingual books derives from ensuring comprehension and using students' background language knowledge. Any problems associated with concurrent translation are avoided with careful planning (Ulanoff & Pucci, 1999). The native language is used as an aid to comprehension and for purposes of analysis by using a bilingual text or two different versions of a book, one in English and one in the native language.

The utility of English books with parallel content lies in teaching ELLs about content by analyzing the similarities and differences among concepts and the ways these are expressed. For example, many nonfiction picture books describe animals using parallel information and language.

The compare and contrast strategy is useful in examining English itself by analyzing links between pictures and text and between different types of text. Picture books are a natural fit for engaging ELLs in discussions about the information conveyed in illustrations, comparing it to the information in the text, and analyzing whether there are strong or weak associations.

Picture books are also useful for teaching ELLs about different styles and genres. ELLs can learn to identify different linguistic and literary devices used in each style. Multilevel and multistyle texts are ideal for this. An example would be a poem in a book that also contains expository text in its end pages. ELLs also benefit from analyzing the different language styles of two books based on the same information and the written word compared to the oral language used in paraphrasing and summarizing it.

Books for Compare and Contrast

A Bug, a Bear, and a Boy (McPhail, 1998) has three parallel main characters.

Bugs for Lunch/Insectos Para el Almuerzo (Facklam, 2002) has bilingual text to compare and contrast.

In the Tall, Tall Grass (Fleming, 1991) has parallel content and phrasing to compare and contrast.

What Do Insects Do?/Que Hacen Los Insectos? (Canizares & Chanko, 2003) has bilingual text to compare and contrast.

Where Do Insects Live?/Donde viven los insectos? (Canizares & Reid, 2003) has parallel content and is a bilingual text.

GRAPHICS

Graphics refers simply to the act of using any kind of graphic device. Each graphic device provides a different opportunity for deepening under-standing of corresponding narratives, descriptions, and explanations (Calkins, 1994). Picture books often feature graphic aids to comprehension, everything from the typical paratext of content books, such as an index or summary matrix, to devices unique to picture books, such as having labeled pictures decorating the inside front and back covers.

Using books with graphic devices is of enormous benefit to school-aged ELLs. They employ these as a means to understand the concepts and to refer back and forth between the concept and means of representing it linguistically or visually. Conscious attention to paratext helps ELLs learn important vocabulary used across academic contexts. For example, many different school subjects require the use of such words as *device, example, graph, graphic organizer, illustration, index, insert, label, legend, map,* and *matrix.* The ELL learns about the concept represented in the graphic device and the associated language. Finally, texts containing graphics and paratext improve oral and written expression as well as reading comprehension.

Ideal books to use with this CLT strategy contain graphics and para-text. Using the books below, ELLs can learn about a classification matrix, labeled diagrams and illustrations, indexes, and glossaries.

Books for Graphics

Actual Size (Jenkins, 2004) contains a classification chart.

Bugs! Bugs! Bugs! (Barner, 1999) uses a classification chart.

Garden Friends (DK Publishing, 2010) has labeled diagrams.

A Luna Moth's Life (Himmelman, 1998) illustrates the life cycle and includes a glossary.

Yucky Worms (French, 2010) has labeled illustrations.

GUESSING GAMES

ELLs engaged in guessing games learn to elicit, confirm, clarify, and identify information while using question-and-answer routines (Allen, 1994; Nation, 2001; Smallwood, 2002). The routines teach ELLs many different linguistic forms used in inquiry. When the routine involves unknown information rather than playful, repetitive practice of questions and answers, it is referred to as an *information gap* task.

Different types of interactive picture books provide a wide range of opportunities to exchange visual, verbal, and experiential information. Some contain only visual and verbal information but provide it in formats that engage readers to search and find answers in visuals or under flaps. The samples below contain text with patterned question-and-answer routines about the physical characteristics of tiny animals.

Books for Guessing Games

Double Delight Bugs (Novick & Hale, 2003) has a lift-the-flap question-and-answer format.

How to Hide a Butterfly and Other Insects (Heller, 1992) has a search and find format.

Who's Hiding in the Garden? (Stewart, 1999) has a lift-the-flap question and answer format.

Wonderful Worms (Glaser, 1994) has end page information organized around questions.

THE LANGUAGE EXPERIENCE APPROACH

ELLs benefit enormously from participating in group language experience approach (LEA) projects because the strategy integrates and reinforces oral and written language using a recursive process (Allen & Allen, 1976; Nelson & Linek, 1998; Nessel & Dixon, 2008). In its purest form, the written material is derived from the students' telling the teacher about their experience and then reading this dictated material. Therefore, LEA does not depend on having a prewritten text. However, picture books are an enormously useful resource when preparing ELLs for the linguistic input. Typically, with ELLs, the books are used to preview and frontload key vocabulary as well as essential phrases. Beginners benefit from using them as scaffolds before, during, and after the dictation.

Ideal books for teaching ELLs with LEA are those with projects, written procedures, and directives. LEA is a popular CLT strategy for several reasons. It provides reading samples within the ELLs' abilities and spheres of experience. They have fun while experiencing tasks together and derive pride from being able to contribute to school and community festivals and events. For example, ELLs can use the books below for illustrating invitations, announcements, banners, and pamphlets, as well as for creating crafts activities such as origami, piñatas, and puppets.

Books for LEA

Crafts For Kids Who Are Learning About Insects (Ross, 2009) has steps for craft projects.

Ed Emberley's Picture Pie (Emberley, 2006f) has steps for circle-based animal illustrations.

Insects: Step-by-Step Instructions for 26 Creepy Crawlies (Fisher, 2007) provides procedures for drawing bugs.

Ralph Masiello's Bug Drawing Book (Masiello, 2004) has procedures for drawing.

MODEL-BASED WRITING

Model-based writing is a popular strategy used to improve expressive language. The model texts guide ELLs until they are capable of more creative writing. The strategy is used to teach writing implicitly as well as overtly (Auerbach, 1999; Kim, 2006). ELLs learn by comprehending the writings of others and by using them as templates for their own writing. ELLs will deeply process a model text by identifying key vocabulary and structures. When they copy and substitute their own words in rewriting the text, they learn about English vocabulary, sentence patterns, and discourse structures. Model-based writing can be coupled with direct teaching of literary devices.

A picture book that is written as a diary, journal, or letter, or that contains a letter from the author to the reader, is useful in teaching these writing forms. Also compatible with this strategy are multitext books. Students can compare and contrast the literary devices. The books below include diaries, narratives, and stories with an added plot summary in the end pages.

Books for With Writing Templates

Aaaarrgghh! Spider! (Monks, 2007) can be used as a template for a first person narrative.

Diary of a Fly (Cronin, 2007) can be used as a template for a diary.

Diary of a Spider (Cronin, 2005) can be used as a template for a diary.

Termite Trouble (Caple, 2005) can be used as a template for a brief plot summary.

Wow, It's Worm! (Caple, 2001) can be used as a template for a brief plot summary.

READER'S THEATER

In reader's theater, students read aloud rather than memorize the character's lines (Harris & Hodges, 1995). ELLs develop speed in tandem with accuracy when they reread books (Cox, 2005). As with other repetitive language learning and fluency tasks, familiarity with a text allows ELLs to focus on developing other skills. For example, the multiple rehearsals of a text in preparation for a reader's theater production helps ELLs develop pronunciation, interpretation, and connections between oral and written forms.

Reader's theater can be the foundation for more open-ended dramatic tasks, such as role-play. In role-play students assume or act out a character without reading prepared lines. Books for reader's theater contain the speech of different characters, first person accounts, familiar tales, and stories about characters with strong distinct personalities.

Books for Reader's Theater

Alien Invaders (Huggins-Cooper, 2010) is a first person story.

Alien Invaders/Invasores Extraterrestres (Huggins-Cooper, 2005) is bilingual.

I'm a Caterpillar (Marzollo, 1997) is a first person story.

I'm a Pill Bug (Tokuda, 2006) is a first person story.

I Love Bugs! (Dodd, 2011) is a young child describing bugs in rhyming couplets.

REALIA

The use of realia is one of the best known vocabulary strategies in CLT. It is a means to directly immerse students in using new words without any translation (Nation, 2001). Direct vocabulary teaching of this kind helps ELLs catch up to their English speaking peers (Calderon, 2007; Hickman & Pollard-Durodola, 2009; Laufer & Paribakht, 1998). Realia is the use of objects, artifacts, and models. It directly involves students in communication about object referents, using new vocabulary in sentences to inquire and exchange information.

Books compatible with realia contain concrete nouns. These include story and concept books about objects as well as books with embedded textures to touch. The realia strategy can expand vocabulary through the use of patterned sentences in which students substitute and fill in words of the same class.

Books for Realia

Crafts for Kids Who Are Learning About Insects (Ross, 2009) has illustrated steps for projects.

Feely Bugs: To Touch and Feel (Carter, 1995) has embedded paper textures.

Five Little Ladybugs (Gerth, 2005a) has embedded ladybugs.

How Many Bugs in a Box? A Pop-Up Counting Book (Carter, 2006) has embedded textures.

Ten Little Ladybugs (Gerth, 2005b) is a poem with embedded bugs.

RECITATION

A number of CLT strategies focus on oral fluency, an essential skill. Poetry recitation provides ELLs with opportunities for oral repetition as a natural consequence of rehearsing for a performance. Rehearsing improves memorization, an essential stepping-stone or scaffold in second-language learning. Memorizing poetic lines frees ELLs to devote attention to developing a host of communicative competencies.

Learning short single poems does not require written text. However, picture book illustrations for each line of text provide a boost to comprehension. Learning the lines of longer poems requires the scaffolds provided by a picture book. Longer poems can be divided into sections for different lessons. They can also be divided among students.

Note that in the appendix, the term *recitation* refers to a CLT strategy. The term *poem* is sometimes used as a marker of language difficulty. This is because many picture books are illustrated poems that are not easily categorized into a stage of beginner-level difficulty.

Poem Books for Recitation

I Like Bugs (Brown, 1999) has short and simple poetic lines.

I Love Bugs! (Sturges, 2005) is a short, simple, rhyming poem.

Ladybugs: Red, Fiery, and Bright (Posada, 2007) is a short poem.

Quick As a Cricket (Wood, 1997) has patterned similes.

Twilight Hunt: A Seek-and-Find Book (Oliver, 2009) is a poetic text about camouflaged animals.

RETELLING

Shared reading of picture books provides students with sustained opportunities to experience the language of storytelling and retelling (Morrow, 1988; Tompkins, 2006). Using retelling with ELLs is different from using it with native English speakers, even when the strategy is to develop skills incidentally. ELLs need to focus on intelligibility, coherence, cohesion, paraphrasing, vocabulary, and summarization. Therefore, teachers add multiple steps using CLT strategies (Calderon, 2007). ELLs benefit from explicit teaching with frontloading of vocabulary, models, graphic organizers, and story frames (Vacca, Vacca, & Gove, 2012; Fowler, 1982). ELLs benefit from being able to rely on a picture book's visual and verbal resources when retelling.

Books with clear text, illustrations, sequential plots, and transparent story lines are ideal. As was described earlier in using a retelling scale for assessment, wordless stories (Russell, 2000) are used to teach oral language. It is important to preplan the language used with a wordless picture book to ensure it is within the ELL's level of ELP.

Books for Retelling

Are You a Ladybug? (Allen, 2000b) tells about the ladybug's life cycle with patterned sentences.

Bow-Wow Bugs a Bug (Newgarden, 2007) is a complex and humorous wordless story.

Well Done, Worm! (Caple, 2000) has a brief outline of the plot on the inside cover.

Wow, It's Worm! (Caple, 2001) has a brief outline of the plot on the inside cover.

TOTAL PHYSICAL RESPONSE AND REENACTMENT

Teaching beginners with actions has been popular for over a century (Gouin, 1892). It paces instruction so beginners can demonstrate comprehension without additionally having to respond in English (Herrell & Jordan, 2003; Lado, 1988). In TPR, ELLs move to the teacher's directives (Asher, 1986). It can be used to introduce the action words in a picture book. Previewing this vocabulary equips ELLs to later understand them within a larger context.

In reenactment, a teacher reads while students dramatically represent the meaning of sentences, scenes, and entire stories. Eventually, TPR and reenactment activities lead to more open-ended tasks. Books for TPR in the following list contain lots of active verbs. Books for reenactment have dramatic scenes and strong characters.

Books for TPR and Reenactment

Are You a Grasshopper? (Allen, 2002) has active verbs, such as *push, eat, lay, struggle,* and *wrap.*

Brilliant Bees (Glaser, 2003) has active verbs, such as *shake, collect, dance, carry, loop, lay,* and *sting.*

Caterpillar Spring, Butterfly Summer (Hood, 2003) has active verbs, such as *eat, sleep, crawl, lay,* and *fly.*

Dazzling Dragonflies: A Life Cycle Story (Glaser, 2008) has active verbs, such as *flip, hide, crawl,* and *fly.*

In My World (Ehlert, 2006) has active verbs paired with nouns, such as *fluttering/moths, creeping/bugs,* and *wiggling/worms.*

VISUALIZING

Visuals are a standard CLT tool for improving comprehension. Beginners use visual scaffolds to make their needs known, recall information, and expand vocabulary. Visualizing is "a process, or result, of mentally picturing objects or events that are normally experienced directly" (Harris & Hodges, 1995, p. 274). It is one of several explicit language-learning strategies used with school-aged ELLs to boost academic language comprehension (Chamot & O'Malley, 1994).

Using visualization as an explicit language-learning strategy, ELLs label illustrations, illustrate words, and match graphic cues to aid comprehension of linguistic forms of communication (Early, 1991; Weber 2009). One of the most common tools of this strategy is a set of vocabulary picture cards used for matching, sentence building, substitution, categorizing, and sorting tasks.

CLT often relies on the use of picture dictionaries organized around semantic categories rather than the alphabet. Grouping items semantically helps with comprehension. Bilingual picture dictionaries are used to tap background knowledge for comprehension and language-focused learning through compare and contrast. In addition to picture dictionaries, wordless concept books can be used as visual props for vocabulary development (Anstey, 2002; Nikolajeva & Scott, 2006; Nolde, 2008; Wolfenbarger & Sipe, 2007). The best books for teaching through visualizing have clear illustrations and provide semantic and sentence context. It is essential in CLT to teach new vocabulary words with examples in sentence contexts.

Books for Visual Strategies

Bugs Are Insects (Rockwell, 2001) contains examples, an index, and key.

Busy Buzzy Bee (DK Reader) (Wallace, 1999) has labeled inserts.

In the Tall, Tall Grass (Fleming, 1991) contains a page for each tiny animal.

Milet Picture Dictionary (Turhan, 2005) has a page of tiny animals.

What Is an Insect? (Canizares, 1998) contains photographs accompanied by phrases.

CONCLUSION

We have reached the last step in the process of finding books with tellability, the necessary search for congruities between the text and the language required by a CLT strategy. Various factors are considered in organizing books to match the 12 CLT strategies mentioned. Some books have many features reflecting just as many factors, and others have just a few. The CLT strategies annotated in the list of tellable books all adhere to the following parameters. They

- represent balance among comprehension, expressive, language-focus, and fluency;
- have topics of interest and familiar to school-aged beginner ELLs;
- cover a balance of linguistic, discourse, strategic, and sociocultural competencies;
- provide for integrated exposure to oral and written skills; and
- have abundant examples of a CLT-compatible feature either across several books or within one book.

The sample CLT strategies presented in this chapter were applied to books about tiny animals. The book samples were found by applying a four-step process, summarized in the questions below.

TELLABILITY IN PRACTICE: MATCHING BOOKS TO CLT STRATEGIES

Select and find one of the books cited in this chapter in your library or bookstore or via digital means. Evaluate it according to the concepts discussed in the chapter based on the questions provided here. Repeat this with a book of your choice from another chapter or resource and analyze it in the same way.

5.1. What features are compatible with a CLT strategy?

5.2. Is it compatible with other CLT strategies?

5.3. Are there enough features congruent with a particular CLT strategy?

Box 5.1   Thematic Book List Covering a Balance of CLT Strategies

COMPREHENSION

Total Physical Response and Reenactment—Books with active verbs and scenes.

Are You a Grasshopper? (Allen, 2002) Stage 4 and intermediate.

Brilliant Bees (Glaser, 2003) Stage 4 and intermediate.

(Continued)

(Continued)

Caterpillar Spring, Butterfly Summer (Hood, 2003) Stage 3. Also for CLT: recitation.

Dazzling Dragonflies: A Life Cycle Story. (Glaser, 2008) Stage 4. Also for CLT: retelling.

In My World (Ehlert, 2006) Stage 1. Also for CLT: visualizing.

Realia—Books with objects and embedded textures.

Crafts for Kids Who Want to Know About Insects (Ross, 2000) Stage 4 and intermediate. Also for CLT: LEA.

Feely Bugs: To Touch and Feel (Carter, 1995) Stage 2. Also for CLT: recitation, visualizing.

Five Little Ladybugs (Gerth, 2005a) Poem not calibrated for stage. Also for CLT: recitation, TPR.

How Many Bugs in a Box? (Carter, 1988) Stage 1. Also for CLT: visualizing.

Ten Little Ladybugs (Gerth, 2005b) Poem not calibrated for stage. Also for CLT: recitation, TPR.

Visualizing—Books for visual scaffolds of vocabulary, dictionaries.

Bugs Are Insects (Rockwell, 2001) Stage 4 and Intermediate. Also for CLT: graphics.

Busy Buzzy Bee (Wallace, 1999) Beginning reader not calibrated for stage. Contains labeled inserts similar to a picture dictionary.

In the Tall, Tall Grass (Fleming, 1991) Stage 2 Also for CLT: compare and contrast.

Milet Picture Dictionary (Turhan, 2005) Picture dictionary.

What Is an Insect? (Canizares, 1998) Stage 1.

EXPRESSION

Retelling—Sequential narratives and expository texts.

Are You a Ladybug? (Allen, 2000b) Stage 4.

Bow-Wow Bugs a Bug (Newgarden, 2007) Wordless.

Well Done, Worm! (Caple, 2000) Stage 2.

Wow, It's Worm! (Caple, 2001) Stage 2.

Guessing Games—Books with question-and-answer routines and oral styles.

Double Delight Bugs (Novick & Hale, 2003) Stage 2.

How to Hide a Butterfly and Other Insects (Heller, 1992) Stage 4.

Who's Hiding in the Garden? (Stewart, 1999) Stage 2.

Wonderful Worms (Glaser, 1994) Stage 2.

Language Experience Approach—Books about experiential tasks.

Crafts for Kids Who Are Learning About Insects (Ross, 2009) Stage 4.

Ed Emberley's Picture Pie (Emberley, 2006f) Wordless illustrations. Project directions are not calibrated for stage.

Insects: Step-by-Step Instructions for 26 Creepy Crawlies (Fisher, 2007)

Ralph Masiello's Bug Drawing Book (Masiello, 2004) Wordless illustrations. Project directions are not calibrated for stage.

LANGUAGE-FOCUSED LEARNING

Model-Based Writing—Books serving as templates, such as a diary.

Aaaarrgghh! Spider! (Monks, 2007) Stage 4. Also for CLT: reader's theater.

Diary of a Fly (Cronin, 2007) Stage 4 and intermediate. Also for CLT: retelling.

Diary of a Spider (Cronin, 2005) Stage 4 and intermediate. Also for CLT: retelling.

Termite Trouble (Caple, 2005) Stage 2. Also for CLT: compare and contrast.

Wow, It's Worm (Caple, 2001) Stage 2. Also for CLT: compare and contrast.

Compare and Contrast—Comparable information, text, and language.

A Bug, a Bear, and a Boy (McPhail, 1998) Wordless.

Bugs for Lunch/Insectos Para el Almuerzo (Facklam, 2002). Stage multilevel.

In the Tall, Tall Grass (Fleming, 1991) Stage 2.

What Do Insects Do?/Que Hacen Los Insectos? (Canizares & Chanko, 2003) Stage 1.

Where Do Insects Live? / Donde viven los insectos? (Canizares & Reid, 2003) Stage 1.

Graphics—Graphic organizers, pictures, and maps.

Actual Size (Jenkins, 2004) Stage 4 and Intermediate. Also for CLT: compare and contrast.

Bugs! Bugs! Bugs! (Barner, 1999) Stage 2. Also for CLT: compare and contrast, recitation.

(Continued)

(Continued)

Garden Friends (DK Publishing, 2010) Stage 3.

A Luna Moth's Life (Himmelman, 1998) Stage 4. Also for CLT: retelling.

Yucky Worms (French, 2010) Stage 4. Also for CLT: reader's theater.

FLUENCY

Reader's Theater—First person dialogue.

Alien Invaders/Invasores Extraterrestres (Huggins-Cooper, 2005) Not calibrated for stage. It is bilingual. Also for CLT: compare and contrast.

I'm a Caterpillar (Marzollo, 1997) Stage 2. Also for CLT: graphics.

I'm a Pill Bug (Tokuda, 2006) Stage 3. Also for CLT: graphics.

I Love Bugs! (Dodd, 2011) Stage 2. Also for CLT: recitation.

Recitation—Books containing a poem.

I Like Bugs (Brown, 1999) Stage 1. Also for CLT: chanting.

I Love Bugs! (Sturges, 2005) Stage 2. Also for CLT: chanting, graphics.

Ladybugs: Red, Fiery, and Bright (Posada, 2007) Poem not calibrated for stage.

Quick As a Cricket (Wood, 1997) Stage 1. Also for CLT: chanting, reenactment.

Twilight Hunt: A Seek-and-Find Book (Oliver, 2009) Stage 4. Also for CLT: graphics, guessing games.

Chanting, Singing—Repetition and lyrics.

The Ants Came Marching (Kelly, 2000) Song.

Beetle Bop (Fleming, 2007) Stage 2. CLT: Also for CLT: compare and contrast.

Hey, Little Ant (Hoose & Hoose, 1998) English/Spanish. Also for CLT: retelling, compare and contrast.

Spider on the Floor (Raffi, 1996). Song.

SUMMARY OF QUESTIONS FOR SELECTING BOOKS WITH TELLABILITY[2]

Chapter 1, Step 1. Finding the right books for CLT

1. What features does the book have that are associated with CLT, addressing each of the following: comprehension, expression, language-focused learning, and fluency development?

Chapter 2, Step 2. Finding books with the right topic

2.1. How difficult or demanding is the content?

2.2. How useful is it?

2.3. How interesting and relevant is it?

Chapter 3, Step 3. Finding books with the right level of difficulty

3.1. What is the amount of language in the text?

3.2. What is the language complexity?

3.3. How much of each is present in the book?

Chapter 4, Step 4. Matching texts to ELLs

4.1. Does the book match student ELP and address listening, speaking, reading, and writing in book-based interactions?

4.2. Does the book match student proficiencies across the linguistic, discourse, strategic, and sociocultural communicative competencies?

Chapter 5, Step 5. Finding books that complement a CLT strategy

5.1. What features are compatible with a CLT strategy?

5.2. Is the book compatible with other CLT strategies?

5.3. Are there enough features congruent with a particular CLT strategy?

NOTES

1. Word class refers to categories of words, such as parts of speech. Two major word classes are (1) *lexical*, such as nouns, verbs, and adjectives; and (2) *function*, such as determiners, particles, and prepositions.

2. It is impractical to calibrate all books into stages, and therefore some will be listed as simply poems, songs, wordless books, multitext, or picture dictionaries.

Concluding Remarks

Years ago, the criteria I used in selecting books was whether my students found it fascinating. Their interest in its topic, images, language, or format was the prevalent criterion. I enjoyed developing materials for book-based communicative language teaching (CLT). Back then, I had much more time to create materials to bridge the divide between the book and their English competence.

Now, I carefully choose picture books to match each student's level of English language proficiency (ELP). Even though I choose from a narrow selection of sparse-text books, the effect is that they learn more language. The English language learners (ELLs) are able to access, practice, and expand their English on their own because the books are within their instructional range.

I love using books with tellability. Finding them requires time examining them and observing beginner ELLs using them, but the benefits are worth the effort. The selection process involves both static and flexible variables. It requires some straightforward analysis of static features, such as the text. It also requires analysis of contextual factors, such as student characteristics.

As outlined in this book, the process of finding the right book begins by examining its features for adherence to CLT principles. The book must support the teaching of comprehension, expression, language-focused learning, and fluency. In addition, it includes determining whether a book's topic and language are also right for ELLs. Finally, the format of the book is examined in order to match it to a CLT strategy. Describing the steps makes the process seem systematic, but finding the right book is also an art. Having an ideal picture book is not sufficient to ensure that beginners are learning English.

Applying these steps is not a flawless way of predicting whether or how a particular picture book creates a language learning opportunity.

We must carefully observe our students interacting with the book and taking guidance from us as they engage in book-based language learning. Here are a few caveats for doing so:

1. Select quality books. Avoid bad literature and books with illustrations of toddlers or that are focused on literacy development.

2. Give ELLs choices within their ELP level. Do not force topics. Their investment helps language learning.

3. Provide books that capture their emotions and imagination. Do not impose rigid ELP limitations. Interest trumps language difficulty.

4. Capitalize on serendipitous connections arising among students, texts, visuals, and experiences. Watch out for rigid planning.

In sum, share the book in ways that make use of your creativity and that of ELLs, authors, and illustrators. Teachable language appears during attention to communication itself.

The appendix that follows is included to provide more examples of teaching beginner ELLs with tellable picture books. It includes three thematic units, each with four lessons. These lessons—with themes of cats, food, and people   cover the 12 CLT strategies and illustrate ways to incorporate the four strands of a balanced program: comprehension, expression, language-focused learning, and fluency. In addition, on the book's website, http://www.corwin.com/picturebooks4ells, there is an electronic list of books that allows selection by such variables as topics, strategies, and stages.

Acronyms and Glossary of Terms

ACRONYMS

CLT communicative language teaching

ELL English language learner

ELP English language proficiency

LEA language experience approach (a teaching strategy)

TESOL teaching English to speakers of other languages

TPR total physical response (a teaching strategy)

GLOSSARY OF TERMS

Academic language refers to the variety of language used in a specific setting. Academic language is the variety that is used across subject matter in a formal school context.

Accommodations are a form of simplification. Teachers simplify language and instruction in ways that increase students' access to grade-level content.

Beginning-level ELLs refers to students who are encountering English for the first time. Students at this ELP level are deeply dependent on the context and teacher in order to engage in communicative interactions. In the United States, the term is used to refer to students within the first year of attending an English-speaking school.

Chanting is a CLT strategy used with repetitive texts. The students engage in oral repetition. Picture books with repetitive text are ideal for this strategy.

Cognates are two words in different languages that have similar meanings and forms.

Compare and contrast is a ubiquitous CLT strategy. Picture books with parallel information, versions in different languages, or other comparable features are ideal for this language-learning strategy.

Communicative competency is the ability to know when, where, and how to use language across contexts and includes linguistic, discourse, strategic, and sociocultural competencies (Canale, 1983; Uso-Juan & Martinez-Flor, 2006).

Comprehensible input is a construct developed to describe language that is understandable to a second-language learner. It includes meaning derived from listening and reading that is within the student's instructional range. It is one of the four basic strands in a balanced CLT program (see Nation, 1996).

Communicative language teaching (CLT) is an approach that is founded on meaningful language usage. It begins with the content and functions of language. Linguistic elements are selected that best serve the communication of such notions in context (Lado, 1988; Nasr, 1994; Nation, 2001). It includes linguistic, discourse, strategic, and sociocultural competencies. In the book lists in the appendix, each listing is followed by one or more specific CLT strategies.

Contextualizing refers to simplifications that provide explanations of meaning through information given within the situation or the words or phrases surrounding it.

Cumulative tale or poem refers to text with successive additions made to a repetitive plot line. ELLs benefit from the repeated pattern.

Dialogue journal refers to written letters back and forth between a student and teacher. The teacher's letters provide a model for student writing as well as personalized feedback to the student.

Dictogloss or Dictoglos is a classroom dictation activity that requires learners to reconstruct a short text by listening and noting key words to use as a base for reconstruction (see Herrell & Jordan, 2012).

Discourse refers to communicative structures and patterns above the sentence level, such as stories, letters, and conversations. Discourse competence refers to the ability to use these linguistic forms and understand the internal structures, such as the structure of a story.

English language learners (ELL) are students who speak a language other than English and are learning English in a school setting.

English language proficiency (ELP) is a complex construct that includes both receptive (listening and reading) and expressive (speaking and writing) skills. It also includes the subsystems of language that together impart meaning (semantics). These aspects are sound, vocabulary, grammar, and discourse systems (Lado, 1988; Nation, 2008).

Extralinguistic refers to aspects of communication that are nonverbal, such as body, hand, and facial gestures and movement.

Expressive output is a construct developed to describe the learner's speaking and writing to convey ideas. It is one of the four basic strands in a balanced CLT program (see Nation, 1996).

Fluency is a language skill that involves accuracy, speed, and proper expression using automatic processing rather than conscious attention. It is one of the four basic strands in a balanced CLT program (see Nation, 1996).

Frontloading is a technique teachers use to simplify language learning by providing essential information and key vocabulary before a lesson begins.

Formulaic speech refers to expressions learned as a whole that are used for particular situations. They are commonly used for teaching students in early levels of language proficiency because they reduce the linguistic demand and at the same time are useful in communication. Examples include unanalyzed chunks, such as "How are you doing?" "See you later" and "I don't know."

Graphics refers to a CLT strategy used to scaffold text. Text graphing refers to students using a graph to outline the text structures. Picture books with maps, matrixes, and other graphic organizers are ideal for applying this CLT strategy.

Graphic organizers are models on which students base their writing, such as story maps and semantic maps.

Guessing games refers to a CLT strategy. It is used with concept books in which questions or information gaps are used to teach the vocabulary and structures used in interchanges about identifying, describing, and analyzing ideas.

Language experience approach (LEA) is a strategy in which text is created by a teacher taking dictation based on the oral language of the students.

The teacher and students explore project-based books as a way to introduce language in a precursor activity to the project.

Language-focused learning is a construct developed to describe deliberate attention to explicit language activities. It is one of the four basic strands in a balanced CLT program (see Nation, 1996).

Learning strategy or language learning strategies are conscious, deliberate routines used to understand, learn, develop, or remember the English being taught (Chamot, 2005).

Linguistic redundancy is inherent in communication. For example, a phrase may include a number word, a plural suffix, and a here-and-now example of the topic, for example, "I have three books in my hands."

Model-based writing is a CLT strategy. It is used with books having templates of discourse structures, such as a diary or a letter, that lend themselves to teaching written expression with guided gradual release tasks.

Morphology is the study of the internal structure of words and word formation. Vocabulary includes the morphology and the units in the lexicon. Words in English are related to other words by rules that English speakers recognize; for example, *dog, dogs,* and *dog-catcher* are closely related (see Nation, 2008; Uso-Juan & Martinez-Flor, 2006).

Multilevel text is a term used to describe picture books that have several texts. I use the term for books with written text at different levels of difficulty.

Multigenre text or **multitype text** is a term used to refer to picture books that contain various texts, such as a poem book with expository end pages.

Paralanguage refers to nonverbal means of communication that accompany speech and convey further meaning, such as tone of voice, pitch, laughter, gestures, and facial expressions.

Paratext is the text outside the space occupied by the text itself, including such features as titles and subtitles, names of authors and illustrators, illustrations, blurbs on the inside cover, reviews, letters to readers, tables of contents, glossaries, and indexes.

Phonology is a subsystem of language, the sounds and sound sequences that make up meaningful units of language. In English, these units are represented in the writing system. Phonemes are the smallest units of words that have the capacity to change meaning, whereas words themselves carry meaning.

Pragmatics studies how people comprehend and produce communication in a concrete situation and compares the differences between different usages, for example, the units appropriate for spoken communication compared to written communication. Contrastive pragmatics studies cultural breakdowns and ways language learners comprehend and develop pragmatic competence over time.

Realia are artifacts, replicas, models, and objects. The term is used here as a CLT strategy in which students use objects (such as a plastic food or model cars). Picture books with embedded textures on their pages (such as scratchy or soft pages) and books about objects are ideal for this strategy.

Reenactment is a CLT strategy in which teachers read sentences or entire scenes, and students dramatically represent the meaning (Herrell & Jordan, 2012).

Reader's theater is a strategy in which students read the speech of the characters aloud. It is used with books with oral text, first person accounts, and dialogue.

Recitation is a CLT strategy. It is used with single poem books, which are ideal for teaching interpretation, memorization, and prepared presentations.

Retelling is a teaching strategy usable with transparent and sequential story structures. The CLT focus is on teaching expression, paraphrasing, and summarizing.

Role-play is a strategy in which students assume the role of or act out a character in a dramatic representation of a book.

Scaffolding refers to providing contextual supports for meaning through the use of simplified language, teacher modeling, visuals and graphics, cooperative learning, and hands-on learning (Ovando, Collier, & Combs, 2003).

Semantic map is a type of graphic organizer used to deepen word knowledge. Essential parts for ELLs are word meaning and usage in a sentence. Word map templates can be found in Yopp and Yopp (2006), Boyd-Batstone (2006), and at http://curry.edschool.virginia.edu/go/readquest/strat/wordmap.html.

Shared reading is an interactive reading strategy. Big books with patterned and repetitious text are often used, so students can easily join in the reading aloud of a picture book, or book with enlarged text, while being guided by a teacher.

Simplification is an adjustment in natural language to the ELP level of ELLs. It is used to scaffold, accommodate, contextualize, and frontload language (Chaudron, 1988; Nation, 2008).

Substitution is a ubiquitous CLT strategy in which a phoneme, grapheme, word, or phrase is replaced by a comparable one.

Syntax is the study of the phrases and structure of sentences. While words are generally accepted as being the smallest units of language that carry meaning, syntax refers to the phrases and sentence structures.

Singing is a CLT strategy used with books with song lyrics and musical scores.

Technical language refers to the use of specific academic terms and styles for a particular content field or subject.

Total physical response (TPR) is a CLT strategy in which students listen to a teacher's commands and respond by gestures and movement without needing to respond by verbal expression (Asher, 1982; Herrell & Jordan, 2012).

Wordless books contain pictures and little or no text but have literary elements. They help ELLs develop oral storytelling, linguistic, and literary skills (Russell, 2000).

Visualizing is a language-learning strategy that uses illustrations and other graphic cues to aid communication (Early, 1991; Weber 2009). Visualizing, or as it is sometimes called, visual scaffolding (see Herrell & Jordan, 2012), occurs when students use salient images for comprehension. They may create mental pictures and use them to understand and appreciate descriptive language, or they can use illustrations to support speech. Examples of books for visualizing are wordless concept books and semantically organized picture dictionaries.

Appendix

Three Units Using the Communicative Language Teaching Strategies

The following 12 picture book–based lessons are examples of each of the 12 communicative language teaching (CLT) strategies. These are woven into three thematic units using books about cats, food, and people, respectively. These themes were selected for practical reasons. Each theme includes some appropriate books for upper grade English language learners (ELLs). Each theme has enough picture books for a unit with the four strands of a balanced CLT program. The three units each include lessons addressing comprehension, expression, language-focused study, and fluency.

Cat Theme

> Total physical response (TPR) and reenactment with *Mama Cat Has Three Kittens* (Fleming, 1998)
>
> Retelling with *Kitten's First Full Moon* (Henkes, 2004)
>
> Guessing game with *Where's the Cat?* (Blackstone & Harter, 2003)
>
> Reader's theater with *A Cat and a Dog* (Masurel & Kolar, 2001)

Food Theme

> Realia with *Feast for 10* (Falwell, 2008)
>
> Language experience approach (LEA) with *One Potato: A Counting Book of Potato Prints* (Pomeroy, 2000)
>
> Compare and contrast with *Eating* (bilingual versions) (Swain, 1999c)
>
> Chanting with *Sweet Potato Pie* (Rockwell, 1996)

People Theme

Visualizing with *Cassie's Word Quilt* (Ringgold, 2004)

Model-based writing with *Dear Daisy, Get Well Soon* (Smith, 2002)

Graphics with *Amelia's Fantastic Flight* (Bursik, 1994)

Recitation with *Honey I Love* (Greenfield, 2002)

Each lesson progresses through presentation of the book, engagement in book-based activities, and expansion to ensure deep language processing. Lessons are labeled in the following ways:

1. In the first phase, presentation, ELLs are prepared with models of the new words. This ensures comprehension of the English used with the text and the CLT strategy.

2. In a second phase, practice, ELLs are guided in controlled activities. This ensures that ELLs interact, assimilate, and learn to express themselves in English.

3. In a utilization and expansion phase, ELLs use the language in a wider context. Games and assessments are included to focus on language development and monitor student progress. Activities specific to upper grade ELLs are included as suggestions and often include more sophisticated language-learning tasks involving writing and other books.

The fact that books on these themes are so varied and plentiful makes it easy to incorporate different CLT strategies into each theme. There are many different books available from which to expand and adapt the themes for ELLs of different abilities and ages. Thus, each lesson ends with a list of tellable books complementing the featured CLT strategy and theme. When practical, books on the two other themes are also included. The annotations refer to the required level of English language proficiency (ELP), the topic, and the compatible CLT strategy. The books, activities, and implementation strategies are meant to be seeds from which you create your own lessons.

ADAPTING TO ELLS IN UPPER GRADES

In each lesson, there are suggested books for a wide range of ages, including some books that are age neutral, annotated as "for all grade ELLs," and others for upper grade and high school–aged students, annotated as "for upper grade ELLs." The latter books are a wonderful springboard for older ELLs who have the ability to comprehend sophisticated topics, analyze differences among genres, and incorporate the use of literary devices into their repertoire of language skills.

Unit About Cats With Four Strategies

Cats are a popular subject of picture books, so it is easy to find books with tellability for communicative language teaching (CLT). This unit on cats uses books with different English language proficiency (ELP) levels and formats. Each lesson includes a list of suggested books for use with the focus CLT strategy. Together the four lessons represent a balanced program with rich, integrated oral and written opportunities for teaching comprehension, expression, language-focused learning, and fluency.

The cat unit begins with a lesson using the book *Mama Cat Has Three Kittens* (Fleming, 1998). Its focus is comprehension, using the total physical response (TPR) strategy to teach listening comprehension of active verbs. The book can also be used with reenactment to teach comprehension of sentences in its dramatic scenes.

The second lesson utilizes the award-winning book *Kitten's First Full Moon* (Henkes, 2004). Its focus is the teaching of meaningful expression through retelling. The sequential plot lends itself to summarizing.

Where's the Cat? (Blackstone & Harter, 2003) is a small board book that focuses on explicit teaching of the syntax used in question-and-answer routines. The book lends itself to the guessing game strategy because the text repeats the title question, "Where's the cat?" The book *A Cat and a Dog* (Masurel & Kolar, 2001), an allegory about friendship, is used for teaching fluency because its first-person text lends itself to the reader's theater strategy.

Two of the featured books on this theme, *Kitten's First Full Moon* and *A Cat and a Dog*, can be used as allegories when teaching high school ELLs. Henke's *Kitten* can be interpreted as the pursuit of a goal and lends itself to introducing high school ELLs to sophisticated words for such concepts as misperception, persistence, and achievement. Similarly, *A Cat and a Dog* can be used to discuss such topics as tolerance, codependence, and coexistence.

TPR AND REENACTMENT WITH
MAMA CAT HAS THREE KITTENS

Mama Cat Has Three Kittens (Fleming, 1998) is a simple story about kittens imitating their mother; it has a Stage 2 level of ELP difficulty. It was selected because it lends itself to teaching comprehension of active verbs with TPR. It also has dramatic scenes compatible with reenactment, which challenges beginners to develop comprehension and auditory memory at the sentence level. The TPR rubric and comprehension check (see Chapter 4) are suggested for monitoring the development of these skills. A sample comprehension check adapted for this story is included here.

Prepare and Model

1. Prepare the following lists of five action verbs from the book's text:
   a. *curl up, nap, stretch, yawn, pounce*
   b. *wash, walk, sharpen, chase, dig*

Also prepare in advance the following lists for when the ELLs are ready to expand to learning nouns and verb phrases:

   c. *paws, wall, claws, leaves, sand*
   d. *washes paws, walks the wall, sharpens claws, chases leaves, digs sand*

2. Conduct a TPR activity with the first five words (list a). Say the words with natural intonation. Do the action and prompt student actions. Repeat, randomly order the verb prompts, add the next verb, and gradually discontinue the physical prompt.

3. Conduct a picture walk of the book and draw students' attention to the five verbs as illustrated.

4. Repeat Steps 2 and 3 with the second list of words (list b).

5. Once the students have mastered these 10 verbs, introduce the phrases from list d, adding *s* or *es* to each verb to create its third person form. Adapt as needed by first introducing the nouns alone (list c.).

6. Conduct a shared reading to teach words for simple directives by showing students the finger actions for the following verbs, and have individual students identify the four characters in the book as you ask them to
   point to Boris
   circle Fluffy

underline Mama Cat

draw a square over Skinny

make an X over Boris

make an X next to _____

Practice and Interact

1. Read and reread the book to allow ELLs to experience and absorb natural cues from sentence context and your intonation, enunciation, and facial expression. Pause on each page while you show the pictures to allow ELLs more processing time.

2. Continue to engage the ELLs by asking individual students to point, circle, and underline words and illustrations.

3. Group students by characters: *Mama Cat, Boris, Fluffy,* and *Skinny.* Reread the book, and allow them to engage in a reenactment of the scenes.

4. Open the book toward you so the students cannot see the illustrations. Read scenes and have students mime a character's actions.

5. Call a student to the front of the class and whisper an action word, or show the student an illustration of an action. Have the student mime the action so classmates can guess the word for the character or action.

6. Conduct a TPR activity using all the words that have been taught.

7. Allow a student to be the teacher and give the verb commands or scene descriptions.

Utilize and Expand

Use the assessments included on page 96 to observe the abilities of individual students.

Brainstorm

Make a set of verb cards to play a brainstorming game. Have students write verbs on cards that are easy to read from a distance. Add to this set of verb cards any of the following suggestions:

- common verbs used in daily activities, for example *eat, drink, sit, wait*
- prepositional phrases, for example *eat at the table, drink at the sink, sit at a desk, wait at the door*
- new verbs from another book, such as *Cleo the Cat* (Blackstone & Mockford, 2000), which contains verbs such as *wake up, yawn, blink, walk, meow,* and *purr*

Once the cards are ready, put them in a pile. Divide the class into two teams, and have teams take turns picking cards from the pile. Team members act out the meaning of the words on their cards, while members of the other team guess the word or phrase on the card.

Word Sort

Use the word cards prepared for the game to categorize words. See suggestions for categories in the word chart below.

Word Chart			
Verbs		*Nonverbs*	*Locations*
walk	pounce	paws	wall
catch	chase	cat	grass
nap	curl up	mama	lap
stand	scratch	claws	sand
yawn	stretch	kittens	

Have students use the list of words in the chart to make patterned sentences, for example

The cat [verb] *on the* [location].

Upper Grade ELLs

Have students search other books for examples of the words they have learned as well as additional thematic words. These can be added to a word chart, word wall, individual student's interactive notebooks, or a semantic word map. The following are suggestions:

- *Cat on Wheels* (Brimner, 2000) is filled with lots of movement, such as *chasing, riding, charging,* and *knocking off.*
- *Black Cat* (Myers, 1999) has lots of verbs, such as *chasing, banging, dancing, ducking, cutting, falling, passing, sipping, sauntering, spilling, throwing,* and *tiptoeing.*
- *Cats Sleep Anywhere* (Farjeon, 2010) lists places to sleep, such as *chair, drawer, lap, shoe, window ledge, piano,* and *box.*

Assess Using a TPR Comprehension Check

This informal assessment is administered much like a spelling test; it is appropriate for ELLs who have prerequisite background skills and dispositions to respond on paper to directions involving circling, numbering, and underlining.

1. Prepare the TPR comprehension check sheet with illustrated items based on the vocabulary encountered in the book. Adapt it for the level of student ability. For example, the earliest level ELL may find distinguishing similar phonemes difficult, such as the 't' and 'th' in *tree* and *three*.

2. With students, review the directives in the TPR comprehension check sheet you have prepared.

3. Read each directive deliberately, clearly, and at a natural pace. Typically in CLT, the teacher reads the items three times. Keep track of the number of repetitions to ensure reliability in subsequent administrations.

A TPR comprehension check for *Mama Cat Has Three Kittens* is shown in the box below.

1. Draw an X above the three.

2. Underline the walking cat.

3. Draw an X below the tree.

4. Circle the kittens.

5. Draw a square around the napping cat.

6. Circle the pouncing cat.

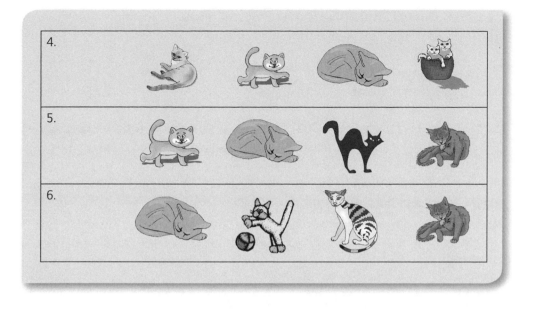

Books for TPR and Reenactment With a Cat Theme

Bad Kitty (Bruel, 2005) Stage 4. Themes: cats, alphabet, animals, food. CLT: TPR.

Black Cat (Myers, 1999) Stage 4. Poem. Theme: cats. Upper grade ELLs. CLT: TPR, recitation.

Cats Sleep Anywhere (Farjeon, 2010) Stage 1. Theme: cats. All grade ELLs. CLT: realia, recitation.

Cat on Wheels (Brimner, 2000) Stage 4. Poem. Theme: cats. Upper grade ELLs. CLT: TPR, reenactment, recitation.

Cleo the Cat (Blackstone & Mockford, 2000) Stage 1. Theme: cats. CLT: TPR, reenactment.

Five Creatures (Jenkins & Bogacki, 2005) Stage 3. Themes: cats, families. CLT: reenactment, chanting.

How to Be a Good Cat (Page, 2011) Stage 3. Theme: cats and dogs. CLT: reenactment.

I Don't Want a Cool Cat! (Dodd, 2009) Stage 1. Theme: cats. Upper grade ELLs. CLT: reenactment, visualizing, chanting.

Just Like You and Me (Miller, 2001) Stage 4. Themes: animals, people. All grade ELLs. CLT: TPR, reenactment, chanting.

Kittens (Kavanaugh & Gurman, 2009) Stage 1. Theme: cats. All grade ELLs. CLT: TPR, reenactment.

Kitty Says Meow! (Ziefert, 2002) Stage 1. Board book for younger ELLs. Theme: cats. CLT: reenactment.

Kittens! Kittens! Kittens! (Myers & Walker, 2007) Stage 2. Poetic. Theme: cats. CLT: reenactment, chanting.

Mama Cat Has Three Kittens (Fleming, 1998) Stage 2. Theme: cats. CLT: TPR, reenactment.

Books for TPR and Reenactment With Other Themes Including: Animals, Food, and People

Clifford Makes a Friend (Bridwell, 2000) Stage 1. Themes: pets, people, friendship. CLT: TPR.

From Head to Toe (Carle, 2003) Stage 1. Themes: animals, people. CLT: TPR, chanting.

In My World (Ehlert, 2006) Stage 2. Theme: animals. CLT: TPR, visualizing.

Matisse Dance for Joy (Rubin, 2008) Stage 1. Theme: people, art. All grade ELLs. CLT: TPR.

Move (Page & Jenkins, 2006) Stage: Multistage. Theme: animals. CLT: TPR.

Stretch (Cronin & Menchin, 2009) Stage 3. Theme: animals. CLT: TPR, reenactment.

Time to Sleep (Fleming, 2001) Stage 3. Themes: animals, seasons. CLT: reenactment.

Pizza Party (Maccarone, 1994) Stage 1. Themes: food, people. CLT: TPR.

RETELLING WITH *KITTEN'S FIRST FULL MOON*

Books with a strong main character and a sequential plot are ideal for teaching expression through retelling. *Kitten's First Full Moon* (Henkes, 2004) is a Caldecott Medal winner with just such characteristics. In the following lesson, the teacher frontloads vocabulary by walking the students through the story line, explaining the main scenes, and teaching key vocabulary. Oral retelling of the story helps them develop paraphrasing and summarizing skills they will use later in writing. Additionally, the lesson helps develop writing skills by applying organizers, such as story frames, graphic organizers, and fold-a-books (see p. 101).

A retelling scale (see Chapter 4) can be used to monitor expressive language development. Achievement of specific objectives for this story can be monitored with a checklist or story frame.

Prepare and Model

1. Frontload by teaching a list of new vocabulary words. For upper grade ELLs, the maximum number of new words per lesson is 20 and minimum is 4. The exact number depends on their ages. Make the meaning clear using the book's illustrations and, for the verbs, using the TPR strategy:

Verbs

close	stretch	open	lick	bang
wiggle	bump	race	pinch	chase
tumble	climb	leap		

Nouns

milk	porch	sky	tongue	step
edge	sidewalk	tree	garden	grass
eield	pond	nose	eyes	mouth
neck	bottom	ears	bowl	moon

2. Conduct a picture walk emphasizing the illustrations of verbs.

3. Prepare a set of 10 key phrases based on the text. Write these phrases on sentence strips. Highlighting different types of words or parts

of a sentence will help ELLs with comprehension. For example, different colored ink can be used to highlight the pronouns, verbs, and nouns in the following patterned sentences:

She tumbled.	She leaped.	She raced.
She chased it.	She licked it.	She climbed it.
She opened her mouth.	She closed her eyes.	She stretched her neck.
She wiggled her bottom.	She bumped her nose.	She banged her ear.

The prepositions and nouns in the following phrases can also be highlighted by using different fonts or capital letters. Have students demonstrate comprehension by reenacting them as you read, or have them take turns giving commands to classmates.

in *the pond*	in *the sky*	by *the pond*
on *her tongue*	on *the porch*	from *the top step*
down *the sidewalk*	down *the tree*	to *the very top*
through *the garden*	through *the grass*	past *the field*
to *the edge*	to *the tallest tree*	

4. Give students the sentence strips to hold as you conduct a second picture walk. Each time you come across a picture related to one of the student's sentences, tell him or her. Read the book again, and tell students to listen carefully and lift up their sentence strips when their sentences are read. As each student holds up a strip, the entire class can repeat the phrase aloud.

Practice and Interact

1. Sit in front of a board or large sheet of paper, and write approximately eight questions to frame the story retelling. These questions will be a resource for later rewriting activities, such as making a minibook using the fold-a-book technique. Adjust the number of questions according to the needs of the ELLs.

2. Reread the book and stop at each juncture to ask the class a question. Model and guide answering the question:

Story Frame Questions	Answers
1. What is this title?	*Kitten's First Full Moon.*
2. Who is the author? Illustrator?	The author/illustrator is Kevin Henkes.
3. Who is the story about?	The story is about a hungry kitten.
4. What is the story about?	Kitten wants a bowl of milk.
5. What happens?	She chases it down the sidewalk.
6. What happens next?*	She chases it by the pond.
7. What happens next?*	She climbs a tall tree.
8. What happens in the end?	She licks milk on the porch.
9. What is your opinion or comment?*	

3. Close the book. Demonstrate retelling the story using the column of answers and referring to the book itself.

4. Pair students to rehearse the retelling and share the story in their own words.

5. Teach the fold-a-book activity, and have students write the story in their own words. This technique involves folding a sheet of paper into eight pages (see http://www.firsthandlearning.org/fold.html). Students fill in the pages as follows and can read them to each other.

    a. Cover page with the title, author, and illustrator.

    b. Inside cover page introduces the main character.

    c. Pages 3–6 include scenes such as these:
       leaped out the window
       leaped past the garden
       climbed a tree
       chased birds
       walked around a fountain
       leaped to my arms

    d. Page 7 concludes with an ending statement, such as "Finally, he fell asleep." Or "What a night!"

    e. Back cover with a comment, such as "That's the amazing story of _____."

Questions marked with * are optional for upper grade ELLs. Other possible questions include those using signal words, such as *first, second, third,* and *finally,* and vocabulary of a more sophisticated nature, such as "What does it want?" "What does it want to achieve?" "What is frustrating?" "What are the barriers?" and "Does it persist?"

Utilize and Expand

Word Hunt

Put students in teams. First, they are to compete to find all the modifiers used in *Kitten's First Full Moon,* such as *black, big, wet, tall, top, bottom,* and *hungry.* As soon as a team finds a noun phrase with such a modifier, all activity stops, and one person in that team (Team A) is to say the phrase aloud, such as *black kitten* or *tall tree.*

The other team (Team B) is given time to think of a substitution word, such as *white, tiny, huge, green, nice,* or *scared,* and make a new phrase. If they think of one, they earn a point. As needed, review the following suggestions:

black kitten -> white kitten,	*tall tree -> tiny tree*
big bowl -> huge bowl,	*wet kitten -> scared kitten*
big bowl -> tiny bowl,	*tall tree -> big tree*
top step -> green step	

Other options:

1. Substitute text sentences to create silly ones, such as the following:
   She closed her mouth (eye).
   She wiggled her ear (nose).
   She bumped her bottom (ear).

2. Expand the list of words about the body in the list, and create sentences using these, such as the following:
   She stretched her (tongue, arm, leg).
   She banged her (knee, shoulder).
   She licked her (lips, teeth).

3. Expand objects, such as in the following examples:
   He tumbled off (the porch, the step, the table).
   He chased (the kitten, the mouse, me).
   He climbed (steps, chairs, shelves).

Upper Grade ELLs

1. List the scenes in the story. Have students brainstorm other places a kitten could go, and add these to the list. Examples include *through the classroom, through the principal's window, past the playground, to the goalpost, with a friend, on a car,* and *past the parking lot.*

2. Search other books for other ideas to add to the list. The following are suggested books for this:

- *Holly: The True Story of a Cat* (Brown, 2000) has examples of activities Holly engages in, such as catching, curling up to sleep, relaxing, and hiding from her kittens.
- *Hondo and Fabian* (McCarty, 2008) has examples of places Hondo and Fabian go, such as on the windowsill, in the car, and to the beach.
- *Six Dinner Sid* (Moore, 2011) has examples of different behaviors in each of the six houses Sid visits.

Have students write a new story using different scenes, characters, or episodes. Use the fold-a-book technique as a way for students to write, illustrate, and share their stories.

Assess Using a Story Frame or Checklist

A story frame graphic organizer is shown in the box below. It can be used as a scaffold for students preparing for a book talk or as a record of student performance. A checklist of items to include in the story frame is included below.

Story Frame

Cover: Title

Inside cover: The author and illustrator _____.

Page 1: Once upon a time, in _____ lived a _____.

Page 2: Its name was _____.

Page 3: It wanted _____.

Page 4: It looked for _____.

Page 5: Finally, it found _____.

Back Cover: What a _____!

Based on the age and ELP level of the ELLs, select an appropriate number of items from the list below to make a checklist to evaluate the story frame. Upper grade ELLs can review each other's stories using the checklist.

title	author	illustrator	beginning
characters	plot	scenes	middle
plot resolution	conclusion	illustrations	end
complete sentences	final comment	beginning	descriptive words

Books For Retelling With a Cat Theme

The Gift of Nothing (McDonnell, 2005) Stage 2. Theme: cats. All grade ELLs. CLT: retelling, reader's theater.

Hey, Tabby Cat! (Root, 2000) Stage 1. Theme: cats. CLT: retelling.

Hondo and Fabian (McCarty, 2008) Stage 4. Themes: cats, friendship. All grade ELLs. CLT: retelling, reenactment.

Holly: The True Story of a Cat (Brown, 2000) Stage 4. Theme: cats. All grade ELLs. CLT: retelling, TPR.

Kitten's First Full Moon (Henkes, 2004) Stage 3. Theme: cats. All grade ELLs. CLT: retelling.

Mouse, Look Out! (Waite, 1999) Stage 4. Poetic. Theme: cats. CLT: chanting, recitation, retelling.

Six-Dinner Sid (Moore, 1991) Stage 4. Themes: cats, people. All grade ELLs. CLT: retelling, reenactment.

Six Dinner Sid: A Highland Adventure (Moore, 2011) Stage 4. Themes: cats, people. All grade ELLs. CLT: retelling.

Sneakers, the Seaside Cat (Brown, 2003) Stage 4. Theme: cats. CLT: retelling.

Storm Cats (Doyle, 2004) Stage 3. Themes: cats, friendship. All grade ELLs. CLT: retelling, reenactment.

Hey, Tabby Cat! (Root, 2000) Stage 1. Theme: cats. CLT: retelling.

Three Little Kittens (Galdone, 1986) Stage 2. Poem. Theme: cats. CLT: retelling, reader's theater.

Wordless Storybooks Including Other Themes: Animals, Food, People

Changes, Changes (Hutchins, 1987) Wordless. Theme: people. CLT: retelling, LEA.

The Lion and the Mouse (Pinkney, 2009) Wordless. Themes: animals. friendship. CLT: retelling.

Noah's Ark (Spier, 1977) Wordless. Themes: people, animals. CLT: retelling.

Pancakes for Breakfast (DePaola, 1990) Wordless. Themes: people, food. CLT: retelling, LEA.

Rain (Spier, 1982) Wordless. Theme: people. CLT: retelling.

The Surprise Picnic (Goodall, 1999) Wordless. Theme: cats. CLT: retelling.

The Wind (Felix, 2012) Wordless. Theme: animals. CLT: retelling, LEA.

GUESSING GAME WITH *WHERE'S THE CAT?*

The guessing game strategy can be used with books with patterned questions and information. Books in which readers must find information in the text or illustrations lend themselves to this strategy. *Where's the Cat?* (Blackstone & Harter, 1996) is just such a book. The text lends itself to explicitly focusing ELLs' attention to the WH (who, what, when, where, why, and how) question structure, specifically, to questions with *where* and to learning prepositions of location (*on, under,* etc.). It also can be used in substitution activities in which ELLs add other content.

Mastery of the book can be assessed with a TPR comprehension check focused on prepositions. This should be modified to reflect the focus of the lesson and the abilities of ELLs. Finally, the dictation provided in the subsequent reader's theater lesson (see p. 114) can be adapted for use in this lesson.

Prepare and Model

1. Read the entire book interactively to ensure comprehension.

2. Stop on each page to draw attention to the objective, such as asking a question with *where* and describing a location with a prepositional phrase.

In this lesson, students also learn to use both WH and *yes/no* questions, such as "Where is the cat?" and "Is the cat under the stairs?"

3. Reread each page and ask students to chime in.

4. Write two lists on the board, prepositions in one and objects or locations in the other. Give students a toy animal or picture of an animal, and tell them to have the animal act out a prepositional phrase created from one of the prepositions and one of the objects or locations. Once they have mastered this, switch the combination of prepositions and objects, and have students reenact these new phrases.

Practice and Interact

1. Add lists of classroom objects and locations to the second column, such as *stool, rug, shelf,* and *box.* Use these to create new sentences.

2. Teach students the *yes/no* question related to locations.

    Where is it? It is under the stairs.

    Is it under the stairs? Yes.

    Is it under the table? No.

3. Take turns having one student stand in front of the class but facing away from them. Have a classmate place a toy cat or cat illustration somewhere. Then the student at the front asks one or two *yes/no* questions, such as, "Is the cat on the teacher's chair? Is it on my chair?" If neither is the location, have the student ask a question with *where*, "Where is the cat?" Once this question is answered have another student take a turn being in front of the class.

4. Have students draw an animal in a specific location. Display these drawings, and ask students questions about them, such as "Where is your lion? Is it near a tree?" Rearrange the drawings on the wall, and then engage students in a think-pair-share activity by posing a question to the class, such as "Where is Maria's cat?" Give them time to think of the answer, allowing pairs of students to consult each other, and then call on an individual to share the answer with the class. Once this is mastered, allow students to play the role of the teacher.

Expand and Review

Play Concentration or Go Fish

Have students make two sets of cards, each with a prepositional phrase of location written on it. In Concentration, they place these face-down on a table. Each student flips two over. The objective is to find two that are the same. When they find a matching pair of cards, they keep it.

In Go Fish, the objective is the same. Each student receives three cards. In turns, students ask a classmate whether she or he has one of their cards. For example, the questioner might ask another student, "Do you have a cat under a table?" If the other student has that card, he or she must give it to the questioner.

Upper Grade ELLs

Upper grade ELLs can use other books with interactive question-and-answer routines. The following books are resources for doing this. Once they have explored these books, they can use them as templates to make similar books of their own.

- *My Cat Tuna* (Reiser, 2001) Questions about the five senses in a lift the flap format.
- *Double Delight Animals* (Novick & Hale, 2002) Questions about animals with answers found under flaps.
- *If Not for the Cat: Haiku* (Prelutsky & Rand, 2004) Haiku riddles about animals.
- *I Like Cats!* (Hubbell, 2004) A rhyming poem.

- *Looking Closely Through the Forest* (Serafini, 2008) One of a series in which a close-up detailed photograph is followed by the full view on the next page.

Assess

Students can make their own TPR comprehension checks and try them on their peers. The example below focuses on the prepositional phrases. For simplicity, students might use a smiley face (☺) to represent the cat.

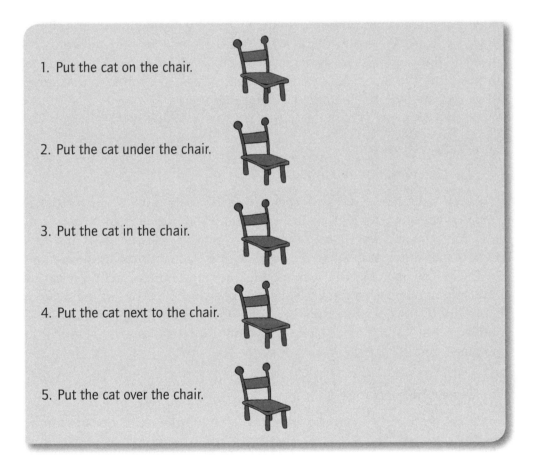

1. Put the cat on the chair.

2. Put the cat under the chair.

3. Put the cat in the chair.

4. Put the cat next to the chair.

5. Put the cat over the chair.

Books for Guessing Games With a Cat Theme

Have You Seen My Cat? (Carle, 1987a) Stage 1. CLT: guessing games.

If Not for the Cat: Haiku (Prelutsky & Rand., 2004) Stage 4. Animal haiku riddles for older ELLs. CLT: guessing games, recitation.

I Like Cats! (Hubbell, 2004) Stage 2 Poem. Interesting for all age groups. CLT: recitation.

My Cat Tuna (Reiser, 2001) Stage 2. Interesting for all age groups. CLT: guessing games.

That's Not My Kitten (Watt, 2001b) Stage 1. CLT: guessing games.

Where's the Cat? (Blackstone &Harter, 2003) Stage 1. CLT: guessing games.

Books for Guessing Games With Other Themes: Animals, Food, People

Apples and Oranges: Going Bananas With Pairs (Pinto, 2008) Poetic. Theme: concept book of interest to all age groups. CLT: guessing games.

Do Pigs Have Stripes? (Walsh, 1996) Stage 2. Themes: humor, animals. CLT: guessing games.

Double Delight Animals (Novick & Hale, 2002) Stage 2. Theme: animals. Use as a template with upper grade ELLs. CLT: guessing games.

Do Crocodiles Moo? (Leslie, 2000) Stage 2. Themes: humor, animals. CLT: guessing games.

Each Orange Had 8 Slices: A Counting Book (Giganti & Crews, 1992) Stage 3. Theme: concept. Interesting to all age groups. CLT: guessing games.

Follow the Line (Ljungkvist, 2006) Stage 4. Theme: people. Interesting to upper grade ELLs. CLT: guessing games.

Follow the Line to School (Ljungkvist, 2011) Stage 4. Theme: people. Interesting to upper grade ELLs. CLT: guessing games.

Follow the Line Through the House (Ljungkvist, 2007) Stage 4. Theme: people. Interesting to upper grade ELLs. CLT: guessing games.

Goodbye, Geese (Carlstrom, 1991) Stage: Poem. Theme: seasons. Upper grade ELLs use as a template. CLT: guessing games, recitation.

I Have Wheels, What Am I? (Crozon, 2000) Stage: Poetic. Bilingual. Theme: concept. CLT: guessing games.

Lemons Are Not Red (Vaccaro Seeger, 2004) Stage 2. Theme: food. CLT: guessing games, visualizing.

Looking Closely Through the Forest (Serafini, 2008) Stage: Multistage. Theme: people. Interesting to upper grade ELLs. CLT: guessing games.

Not a Box (Portis, 2006) Stage 3. Theme: animals. CLT: guessing games, LEA.

Nothing Like a Puffin (Soltis, 2011) Stage 4. Themes: animals, birds. Upper grade ELLs can use as a template. CLT: guessing games.

Tomorrow's Alphabet (Shannon, 1999) Stage 1. Theme: concept. Interesting to upper grade ELLs. CLT: guessing games.

Who Hoots? (Davis, 2004) Stage 1. Theme: animals. CLT: guessing games, reenactment.

Who Hops? (Davis, 2001) Stage 1. Theme: animals. CLT: guessing games, reenactment.

Who Uses This? (Miller, 1990) Stage 1. Theme: people. CLT: guessing games.

What's What: A Guessing Game (Serfozo & Narahashi, 1996) Stage 3. Themes: animals, people. CLT: guessing games.

READER'S THEATER WITH *A CAT AND A DOG*

A Cat and a Dog (Masurel & Kolar, 2001) is essentially an allegory about tolerance, friendship, and interdependence. Its text works well with reader's theater and can be a springboard for more open-ended tasks, such as a role-play. A graphic organizer is used to scaffold writing other versions for other dramatic performances. Upper grade ELLs can use it as a template for writing their own allegories.

Monitor the achievement of oral objectives by adjusting the retelling scale from Chapter 4. An example is included. Also included is another assessment tool, a dictation that can be administered pre- and posttest to literate ELLs. Dictation is scored based on errors of ELP (rather than on spelling), such as word substitutions, omissions, additions, and illegible writing.

Present and Model

1. Conduct a picture walk through *A Cat and a Dog* with the students, and monitor their comprehension. Ask questions about the characters. The story has three characters, including a dog, a cat, and a narrator.

2. List words for emotions, feelings, or moods depicted in the story as the cat and dog play, lose a toy, are mean, and become friends; such words include *happy, sad, excited, angry, sleepy, calm, hungry, jealous,* and *friendly.*

3. Model emotion and the use of intonation as a means of communicating meaning. Have students repeat lines of the text with proper intonation. Have one student dramatize an emotion as expressed by an animal, and have the class guess the animal and the emotion.

4. Make a chart such as the one below with individual columns for questions, statements, and direct speech from the text. Have students add to the columns, and then use these to practice the different intonations.

Questions	Summary	Intonation Practice
What is this title?	*The book title is __.*	Serious
Who is the author? *The author/illustrator is Kevin Henkes.*	*It is written by __.*	Serious
Who was angry? *The story is about a hungry kitten.*	*The dog was angry.*	The dog said, "grrr."
Who was sad?	*The cat was sad.*	The cat said, "nothing."
Who had an idea?	*They thought of something.*	The dog said, "Nothing?"

Practice and Interact

1. Divide the class into narrators, dogs, and cats. Have the narrators, dogs, and cats each write their respective text from the book on sentence strips. Have groups practice saying these phrases aloud to each other. Then have the groups trade strips and practice saying the other phrases aloud as well.

2. Post sentence strips randomly across a wall. Read one sentence. Call on a student to identify whether the speaker in the sentence is the cat, the dog, or the narrator. Continue until all are identified. Switch roles and have a student read one and other classmates identify it.

3. Have students read the book aloud with increasing speed, accuracy, and intonation.

4. Conduct a dramatic rendition of the book for an audience.

Expand and Utilize

Play Snowball

Pair students and have each make a labeled picture of a character on half a paper. On the other half they are to write a line spoken by that character in a speech bubble. Cut the papers in half and bunch each into a snowball. Together, throw these snowballs into the air. Each student picks up one random snowball, opens it, and reads it aloud. Students are to find the person with the matching snowball.

Upper Grade ELLs

Help students work in groups to rewrite the cat and dog story using human characters. The graphic organizer below can be used as a scaffold to outline the story and write dialogue. The left column is for listing scenes and the right for planning the dialogue in each.

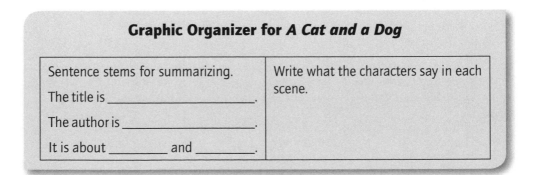

Graphic Organizer for *A Cat and a Dog*

Sentence stems for summarizing. The title is _____. The author is _____. It is about _____ and _____.	Write what the characters say in each scene.

Scene	
Scene	
Scene	
In the end _____	

The following tales of friendship can be used to inspire the writing of scripts for reader's theater.

- *Buster* (Fleming, 2008), also a cat and a dog.
- *Cat and Mouse in the Rain* (Bogacki, 1997), a cat and a mouse.
- *Hondo and Fabian* (McCarty, 2008), a cat and a dog.
- *The Gift of Nothing* (McDonnell, 2005), a cat and a dog.
- *Top Cat* (Ehlert, 1998), two cats.

Assess

Adapt the retelling scale to accommodate the parameters of reader's theater. The following is an example:

Example of a Reader's Theater Assessment

Name:_____ Book Title:_____

Time allotted for rehearsal _____

Comments:

____ Stage 1 Participates without reading, such as repeating a formulaic line, introducing scenes with a placard, reenactment.

____ Stage 2 Limited intelligibility, such as beginner-level pronunciation, intonation, rhythm, and hesitancies. Performance is limited to one character.

____ Stage 3 Intelligible but contains a number of beginner-level pronunciation, intonation, and stress flaws.

____ Stage 4 Oral reading is text-bound but fluent and intelligible.

Dictation

1. Select a passage of the story or a few sentences to use as a dictation. Number each of the phrases. Here are some examples:

    1. A cat and a dog lived in a house.

    2. The cat said, "Nasty dog."

    3. The dog said, "Stay away."

    4. The dog got the cat's toy.

    5. The cat got the dog's ball.

2. Give students a blank page with a large left margin and the numbers for each of the phrases listed in a column. Read the entire passage once. Allow students to take notes in the left margin.

3. Read it again, pausing between phrases, and allowing students time to write what you have dictated for each numbered phrase; prompt as needed.

4. Read it a third time to allow students to silently review and self-correct.

For the earliest beginners and struggling students, you can provide partially completed sentences, sentence stems, or a word bank. An example is included below.

Word Bank	Name: _____ Date: _____
	Book: _____
cat, cat's, dog's dog, got, house how, nasty, the, nicely, stay, toy, ball, day, away	1. A _____ and a _____ lived in a _____. 2. The cat said, _____. 3. The dog said, _____. 4. The dog _____. 5. The cat _____.

Books for Reader's Theater With a Cat Theme

Buster (Fleming, 2008) Stage 4. Theme: friendship, map. CLT: graphics.

A Cat and a Dog (Masurel & Kolar, 2001) Stage 3. Themes: cats, friendship. Interesting to older ELLs. CLT: TPR, reader's theater.

Cat the Cat, Who is That? (Willems, 2010) Stage 1. Theme: animals. CLT: reader's theater.

Cat and Mouse in the Rain (Bogacki, 1997) Stage 3. Theme: friendship. CLT: retelling, reader's theater.

Curious Kittens (Volkmann, 2001) Stage 3. Themes: animals, cats. Interesting to all age groups. CLT: reader's theater.

Cat Is Sleepy (Kitamura, 1996) Stage 1. Themes: animals, cats. Spanish version available. CLT: reader's theater.

Feathers for Lunch (Ehlert, 1996a) Stage 4. Themes: animals, cats. Interesting to all age groups. CLT: TPR, reader's theater.

Hondo and Fabian (McCarty, 2008) Stage 4. Themes: cats, friendship. All grade ELLs. CLT: retelling, reenactment.

Top Cat (Ehlert, 1998) Stage 4. Theme: friendship. Interesting to all age groups. CLT: reader's theater.

Tiger on a Tree (Ravishankar, 2004) Stage 2. Theme: Indian folktale. CLT: chanting, TPR, reader's theater.

Books for Reader's Theater With Other Themes: Animals, Food, People

Catch That Goat! (Alakija, 2005) Stage 2. Theme: people. CLT: realia, reader's theater.

The Chick and the Duckling (Ginsburg, 2000) Stage 2. Themes: animals, friendship. CLT: TPR, reader's theater.

Dinosaurs (Guettier, 2005) Stage 2. Themes: animals, food. CLT: reader's theater.

The Doorbell Rang (Hutchins, 1986) Stage 2. Themes: food, people, mathematics. Interesting to all age groups. CLT: reader's theater.

Happy Belly, Happy Smile (Isadora, 2009) Stage 3. Themes: food, people. CLT: reenactment, reader's theater.

Hattie and the Fox (Fox, 1983) Stage 3. Theme: animals (farm). CLT: reader's theater.

Just Like a Baby (Havill, 2009) Stage 4. Theme: family. CLT: TPR, reader's theater.

Let's Do Nothing (Fucile, 2009) Stage 4. Theme: family. CLT: reader's theater.

Look What I Can Do (Aruego, 1988) Wordless. Theme: friendship. CLT: retelling.

Ten Apples Up on Top (Seuss, 2004) Stage 2. Themes: animals, counting, food. CLT: reader's theater.

The Pigeon Finds a Hot Dog (Willems, 2004) Stage 3. Themes: humor, animals, friendship, food. CLT: reader's theater.

Unit About Food With Four Strategies

Picture books about food are fun to use with beginning English language learners (ELLs) for several reasons. Foods are easy to illustrate, label, and describe. Students can use their background knowledge. There are connections to content subjects, such as kitchen math and measurement.

The following four lessons cover a balance of communicative language teaching (CLT) strategies. The comprehension lesson is based on the book *Feast for 10* (Falwell, 2008). It is a simple story of a family buying groceries and preparing a meal that lends itself to teaching comprehension with realia.

One Potato: A Counting Book of Potato Prints (Pomeroy, 1996) lends itself to teaching expression for two reasons. Its running text is a counting poem that can be recited. The end pages are directions for a vegetable printing project and can be used with the language experience approach (LEA).

Eating (Swain, 1999c) is one of a series of four short bilingual books usable with language-focused learning and the compare and contrast strategy. ELLs can learn to compare and contrast the text and the content. The book has rich photographs of people from across the globe, a world map, bilingual text, and end pages. ELLs can find similarities and differences among cultures, languages, and text formats.

Sweet Potato Pie (Rockwell, 1996) is a beginning reader with a rhythmic and repetitive text. It is useful for developing oral fluency because students engage in unison activities, such as chanting and choral reading.

Each of the four lessons includes suggested activities and books for upper grade ELLs. The topic of *Feast for 10* is age neutral, a family gathering to share a meal. The printing project in *One Potato: A Counting Book of Potato Prints* requires ELLs to be able to make vegetable prints. All four books in Swain's series can be used in a discussion of universal cultural themes and to teach map skills. Finally, the characters in *Sweet Potato Pie* are school aged.

REALIA WITH *FEAST FOR 10*

Feast for 10 (Falwell, 2008) is a simple story told almost as a sequence of labeled illustrations, as family members gather ingredients and prepare a meal. It is ideal for teaching vocabulary with realia because the food items are easy to obtain. Students learn by manipulating, labeling, and making word cards for them. The word cards can be used in sorting and sentence substitution activities.

It is easy to monitor language development while observing ELLs using realia. This lesson includes a survey that can be used as a record of students' developing abilities. Other suggested ways to monitor their growing ability to follow directions include using a total physical response (TPR) rubric or developing a comprehension check.

Prepare and Model

1. Select an instructionally sound amount of realia from the vocabulary of the book. Add variety of items, for example, two items of different sizes or colors, such as big and small, green and red apples. For the youngest and earliest stage ELLs, start with four nouns and four modifiers; with older and later stage beginners, start with ten.

2. Make a book box (Yopp & Yopp, 2006) for items. Have ELLs decorate the sides with pictures of food items.

3. Divide the students into small groups, and give each group two or three objects. They are to make illustrated label cards for each. Place the objects on the cards. Have students repeat the names as they place each one in the box.

4. Model requesting objects from the box using patterned sentences. Expand to sentences for exchanging and replacing objects. Suggested patterns include the following:

> *Is the _____ in the box?*
>
> *Can I have _____?*
>
> *Please put the _____ on the table.*
>
> *Can you pass _____?*
>
> *What do you want?*

5. Add more items to include all those in the book, other items students like, or items for which you have found relevant realia.

Practice and Interact

Before rereading the book, give each student an object from the box to hold.

1. As you read the book, when you mention each student's object, the student is to raise it up.

2. Reread the book interactively, commenting, asking questions, and reviewing scenes to teach additional words and phrases (a list follows). Have students make word cards for attributes, and use sorting activities as well as cloze sentences (Gunderson, 2009, p. 131). Suggestions include the following:

Shape: *round, long, big, oval, oblong*

Taste: *tasty, sweet, sour, salty, good, bad*

Texture: *smooth, cold, hard, soft, leafy*

The big pumpkin is hard and round. How does it feel?

Is ____ a shape or a color?	*Is ____ how it tastes or feels?*
What color is ____?	*What shape is ____?*
Who likes ____?	*What do you like?*
Do you like ____ or ____ better?	*Do apples taste sweet?*

3. Play a circle game. Sit in a circle. Start the game with a noun phrase from the book, such as saying, "two pumpkins." Using the attributes list, model an expanded noun phrase, and emphasize it with intonation as follows:

*two pumpkins -> two **round** pumpkins*

Ask a student to your right to repeat the phrase and switch the attribute.

*two round pumpkins -> two **big** pumpkins*

This student then asks the student to her or his right to continue.

*two big pumpkins -> **three** big pumpkins*

Continue around the circle. When ELLs are stuck for ideas, a buddy can help.

What About You? Role-Play

1. Plan a picnic with the class, and allow students to contribute ideas for foods to include, consulting a picture dictionary.

2. Have students list the items, price them, make labels, and place the items on the table/store.

3. Have students select roles—planner, cook, buyer, and store clerk—and role-play planning the menu, buying the food, and preparing it.

Utilize and Expand

Play a Guessing Game: What Am I Thinking?

Start with a review of the attributes of each object in the book, for example, the pumpkin is orange, large, and round, and it begins with the letter *P.*

Have a student stand in front of the class, select one object from the book, and tell only the teacher which item has been selected.

This student describes one attribute and calls on someone to guess the object. If the guess is correct, the student who guessed goes to the front of class and repeats the activity. If the guess is incorrect, another attribute is described, and another classmate guesses. This continues until someone guesses what the object is.

Upper Grade ELLs

Have students find words for other foods and their attributes in other books. Review these together using the books as a resource. Then have them write the names on individual cards.

Randomly place these cards facedown on a table. Form two teams. Each team is to pick a card and race the other team to write three attributes about the item on the board.

Useful alphabet books for this include the following

- *Eating the Alphabet* (Elhert, 2004) labels them in capital and small letters.
- *Lunch* (Fleming, 1992) lists them in a sequential story.
- *On Market Street* (Lobel, 1989) includes foods as illustrations for some of the letters, for example, *A* is illustrated with apples and *O* with oranges.

Survey[1]

Select fruits or vegetables for focused study of questions using the word *do.* Have students learn the focus questions by using them to survey classmates. Adjust a graphic like either of those shown below to the student's English language proficiency (ELP) level. Have ELLs use it as a scaffold.

Question: Do you like red or green apples?	Apple survey answers
First person I surveyed _____	
Second person I surveyed _____	
Third person I surveyed _____	
Fourth person I surveyed _____	

Questions: Do you like apples? Do you like bananas?	Tally of "like"	Tally of "do not like"

3. Guide ELLs by writing sample questions and demonstrating ways to conduct a survey, and record information on the graphic being used. As needed, review new words, such as *survey, tally, question, results,* and *report.*

Possible questions include the following:

Do you like ___ or ___? Do you like ___? Do ___ taste sweet?

Do you think this ___ tastes sour?

Upper grade ELLs can be shown ways to analyze and summarize the results. Possible report statements include the following:

In my survey I asked, "Do you like apples?

I asked ___ students. I found ___ people liked red apples.

Allow ELLs to select items of their choice for the survey. Review their work, and have them report orally about it.

Assess

Record anecdotal observations of students as they conduct the survey. Develop a comprehension check using illustrations of the items taught.

Books for Realia With a Food Theme

The Apple Pie Tree (Hall & Halpern, 1996) Stage 3. Poem. Theme: food. CLT: LEA, chanting.

Bread, Bread, Bread (Morris, 1993a) Stage 2. Theme: people. Photo index and map. CLT: realia, compare and contrast.

A Cool Drink of Water (Kerley, 2002) Stage 2. Theme: people. CLT: realia, compare and contrast, chanting, graphics.

Dim Sum for Everyone (Lin, 2003) Stage 3. English/Chinese. Themes: food, index. CLT: realia, reenactment, compare and contrast.

Eating the Alphabet (Ehlert, 1989b) Stage 2. Theme: food. Capital and small letters. CLT: realia, visualizing.

Feast for 10 (Falwell, 2008) Stage 1. Theme: food. CLT: realia.

Hold the Anchovies! A Book About Pizza (Rotner & Hellum, 1996) Stage 3. Theme: food. CLT: realia, TPR, LEA.

How to Make an Apple Pie and See the World (Priceman, 1994) Stage 4. Theme: food. CLT: realia, LEA, graphics.

Lunch (Fleming, 1992) Stage 2. Theme: animals. CLT: realia, reenactment.

On Market Street (Lobel, 1989) Stage 1. Theme: alphabet. CLT: realia, visualizing.

Strawberries Are Red (Horacek, 2001) Stage 1. Theme: food. Board book. CLT: realia, visualizing.

We're Going on a Picnic (Hutchins, 2002) Stage 2. Themes: humor, animals. CLT: realia, reader's theater.

Books for Realia With a People Theme

My Backpack (Bunting & Cocca-Leffler, 2005) Stage 4. Theme: people. CLT: realia, retelling.

The Bag I'm Taking to Grandma's (Neitzel & Parker, 1998) Stage 3. Theme: people. CLT: realia, chanting.

The Dress I'll Wear to the Party (Neitzel & Parker, 1995) Stage 3. Theme: people. CLT: chanting, realia.

The Eye Book (Seuss & Mathieu, 1999) Stage 2. Theme: people. CLT: realia.

The Jacket I Wear in the Snow (Neitzel & Parker, 1994) Stage 3. Theme: people. CLT: chanting, realia.

LEA WITH *ONE POTATO: A COUNTING BOOK OF POTATO PRINTS*

One Potato: A Counting Book of Potato Prints (Pomeroy, 1996) has simple and patterned text of noun phrases. Each page has the illustration of a fruit or vegetable. The number of items illustrated on each page increases by 1 until there are 10 items, and then the number increases by 10s up to 100. The end pages describe the procedure for making vegetable prints. This type of project lends itself to LEA. I like to write the basic directions on a chart before embarking on reading those in the text.

Monitoring of the objective of the lesson can be done throughout the LEA activities. A comprehension check and a dictation can be developed for use with LEA. Included here is an example of a dictogloss to be used after the project with upper grade ELLs.

Preparation and Modeling

1. Read the text and encourage students to repeat after you. This text is easily memorized and students should be able to recite it after a few readings.

2. Model using this vocabulary in sentences, and have students practice the intonation and stress structure of natural speech.

   What is this number? The number is 10.

   Can you point to _____? Yes, here is _____.

   Can you find _____? I found _____.

3. Show students the end pages with directions for a printing project. Review the basic steps by writing them on a chart and reading them aloud. Adjust to their ELP level.

4. Gather objects needed for the printing project. Make vocabulary cards for the items, and engage students in talking about them, such as asking questions.

   What do you have?

   Where is the paper?

   Who needs ink?

5. Engage in a printing project. During this experience, continually use and expect ELLs to use key words and sentences, and add additional language items as warranted.

6. Either as they work or after the printing is complete, engage in a guessing game to practice vocabulary. Ask students to guess the names of

vegetables and other objects you describe for them. Allow students to lead the guessing game. Here are some examples:

> *It is long. It is orange. What is it? (carrot)*
>
> *These grow underground. What are they? (carrots and potatoes).*
>
> *It is a colored liquid. What is it? (ink)*
>
> *It begins with the letter 'p.' What is it? (potatoes, paper, print)*

Practice and Interaction

1. Create groups of up to seven students.

2. Use a large sheet of chart paper for this activity, and title it, "Making Prints."

3. Invite each student to share her or his experience. Provide suggestions and have them consult the book, their prints, and each other as much or as little as needed.

4. For each student, transcribe one of the sentences he or she has spoken. Write using standard English punctuation for quotations. Have everyone read the sentence aloud.

5. Reread the chart together, and guide them toward intelligible pronunciation.

6. Follow up by having them use the text of the chart in any of the following ways:

- Read their contribution and that of a friend.
- Copy, personalize, or summarize the story into a journal.
- Cut the story into a series of sentences, scramble them, and reorder them.
- Write the chart as a cloze activity with blanks (Gunderson, 2009, p. 131). Give to a classmate to fill in.
- Compare this chart to the directions in the book or to the teacher's original one.

Expand and Utilize

Make a Food Picture Dictionary

Brainstorm favorite foods. Put foods into semantic categories (vegetables, fruits, dinners, grains, dairy, etc.). Have students copy the words for each category onto a page, illustrate each word, and write a sentence about the category. Gather the pages into a picture dictionary.

Games With Role-Play

1. Plan to have an imaginary pie-eating contest. Divide the class into groups. Each is to select a pie and list the ingredients.

2. Set up an area, such as a desk, to serve as a store. Make cards for all the ingredients, and put the cards in the store.

3. Have each student take a role as a buyer, a cook, or a store clerk.

4. Once the buyer has role-played buying the items (and the store clerk has role-played selling them), the cook must role-play tasting the items to ensure they have the right quality. Any item not just right must be returned to the store, and one with the right quality must be brought back.

Upper Grade ELLs

Students can search how-to-draw books for foods. Use these to play "Picture This" by having students teach each other to draw foods.

1. Have students make step-by-step drawings of foods—such as an orange, grapes, a banana, and an apple. During this experience, provide oral language models, such as *circle/line, under/over, one quarter, one half, right/left,* and *inside/outside.*

2. Give students directions to draw a picture without telling them what they are drawing. Here is an example of directions for drawing a bunch of grapes:

- First, make three circles in a line.
- Second, make two more under it.
- Third, make one more circle under those two.
- Fourth, draw a stem on the top.
- Fifth, draw a leaf on the stem.

Then ask students, "What fruit did you make?"

Assess Using Dictogloss

Use dictogloss to monitor the ability of upper grade ELLs to paraphrase and summarize. The procedure described below is a group activity. ELLs take notes as they listen to a text and write the story in their own words. After this prewriting activity, with its opportunities for verbal interaction and teacher feedback, all students write their own final drafts. You can photocopy the reproducible below and have students write their notes, their drafts, and their final versions on it.

1. Prepare. Select a few sentences from the book. The number will depend on the ages and ELP levels of the ELLs. Read and briefly review key words.

2. Review. Read the passage a second time. Call on students to write a key word on the board, and then allow pairs of students to talk about the words.

3. Listen. Read the passage a third time while students record key words and phrases. Have them work with a partner to review their notes and begin writing the text. The partner should make one constructive comment that each student must incorporate into a second draft.

4. Summarize. Have individual students reconstruct the passage. After you have read it and scored it, allow each student to paste the passages into her or his interactive notebook. Over time, in these notebooks, they will be able to see their progress.

Dictogloss

Name: Date:	Title of Book:

1. Key words heard

2. Phrases heard

3. Additions from review with a partner

4. Draft with a partner

5. My summary

Books for LEA With a Food Theme

Apple Farmer Annie (Wellington, 2001) Stage 4. Themes: food, people. CLT: LEA, retelling, realia.

The Apple Pie That Papa Baked (Thompson, 2007) Stage 2. Themes: food, family. CLT: LEA, chanting.

Build a Burrito: A Counting Book in English and Spanish (Vega, 2008) Stage 2. Theme: food. CLT: LEA, chanting.

The Cooking Book: 50 Mouthwatering Meals and Sensational Snacks (Bull, 2002) Stage 4. Theme: food. CLT: realia, LEA.

Let's Make Pizza (Hill, 2002) Stage 2. Themes: food, people. CLT: LEA.

Mystery Vine: A Pumpkin Surprise (Falwell, 2009) Stage: Multistage. Themes: food, people. CLT: LEA.

A Pie in the Sky (Ehlert, 2004b) Stage: Multistage. Themes: food, people. CLT: LEA, retelling.

Pizza at Sally's (Wellington, 2006) Stage 4. Themes: food, people. CLT: visualizing, LEA.

Today Is Monday in Louisiana (Downing, 2006). Stage: Multistage. Themes: food, people. CLT: LEA, compare and contrast.

We're Making Breakfast for Mother (Neitzel, 1997) Stage 3. Themes: food, family, humor. CLT: chanting, realia, LEA.

Books for LEA With a Crafts Theme

123 I Can Make Prints (Luxbacher, 2008) Stage 4. Theme: crafts. CLT: LEA.

Ed Emberley's Picture Pie (Emberley, 2006f) Stage: Wordless. Theme: crafts. CLT: LEA.

The House I'll Build for the Wrens (Neitzel, 1997) Stage 4. Themes: crafts, people. CLT: LEA, realia.

Kite Flying (Lin, 2004) Stage 1. Themes: family, crafts. CLT: LEA, retelling.

Meow and the Big Box (Braun, 2009) Stage 2. Themes: animals, crafts. CLT: LEA.

Piñata (Emberley, 2004). Stage: Multistage. Spanish and English. Theme: people, crafts. CLT: LEA, compare and contrast.

COMPARE AND CONTRAST WITH *EATING*

Eating (bilingual versions) (Swain, 2000c) is my favorite of Swain's Small World series because of its topic. All four in the series are easy to use for comparing and contrasting parallel ideas, text, and different languages. The parallel ideas are presented in the photographs of people from around the world. These photographs are repeated in an index with more detailed information. This presents opportunities to compare and contrast two types of text. Finally, because it comes in many bilingual versions, such as in English combined with Arabic, Bengali, Chinese, Gujarati, Punjabi, Turkish, Urdu, and Vietnamese, it can be used for learning about English through contrastive analysis.

Monitoring progress in language-focused tasks can be accomplished with anecdotal notes based on observations of students. This lesson includes a semantic map that can be scored, for example, by assigning points for correct words and sentences.

Prepare and Model

1. Build background with a picture walk to connect the theme with student background knowledge.

2. Ask students to role-play being your teacher and teach you several words in their language based on the photographs and text.

3. Model language-learning strategies. Observe your students' responses as you intentionally make mistakes to allow them to teach and correct you. Use any of the following language-learning strategies:

- Make word cards and sentence cards.
- Rehearse and substitute words.
- Test yourself.
- Compare and contrast another language with English.
- Repeatedly ask for help and clarification. For example, if you are learning Turkish, *Am I saying it right? How do you say it? Is it, "Yemeden"? Show me. Where is "Yemeden" in the book? Is the phrase, "Bana yemeden" correct?*

Practice and Interact

1. Switch roles, and teach the students to apply these language-learning strategies to English.

2.   Conduct a second picture walk through the text describing objects in the pictures: "This is a ____. It is red." Depending on their ages and abilities, engage ELLs in sharing a similarity or a difference, substituting, and expanding the descriptions.

3.   Once you are finished with modeling language learning, have each student make a semantic map of a new word, as shown in the box below. Assign each word to two students, so there will be two semantic maps for each word for playing Concentration. The suggestion below contains an illustration, several related words, two sentences, and a translation.

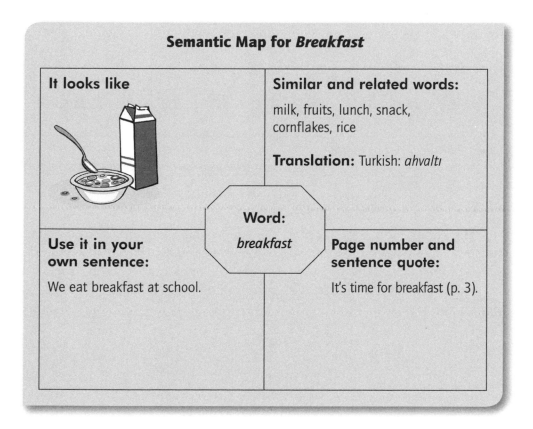

Semantic Map for *Breakfast*

It looks like	**Similar and related words:**
	milk, fruits, lunch, snack, cornflakes, rice
	Translation: Turkish: *ahvaltı*

Word: *breakfast*

Use it in your own sentence:	**Page number and sentence quote:**
We eat breakfast at school.	It's time for breakfast (p. 3).

4. Play Concentration by placing semantic maps upside down on a table. Students are to turn over two. If they are both for the same word, the students keep them. If not, they must turn them back over.

5. Use the new vocabulary. Have students select a new food, either a favorite or one found in another book, and draw themselves eating it. Have them label the food, and write their names and a description of the food on the drawing. Gather these drawings and display them together.

6. Make a picture dictionary for the class with the new words. Have students work with a partner to preview the displayed drawings and organize them by concepts.

Expand and Utilize

Have upper grade ELLs survey their classmates as to their book preferences. The graphic organizer below is just one way for them to organize this activity.

Books Consulted	Did you like __? Yes	Did you like __? No
If You Give a Mouse a Cookie by Numeroff		
If You Give a Cat a Cupcake by Numeroff		
Eating by Swain		
Bread, Bread, Bread by Morris		

Assess Using a Semantic Map

The sample semantic map[2] in the example above contains the essentials for ELLs—word meaning and usage in a sentence. It may also include some of the following: a drawing, translation, book quotes, and associated concepts. You can score it by assigning points to each section, such as 20 points per area.

Your name:

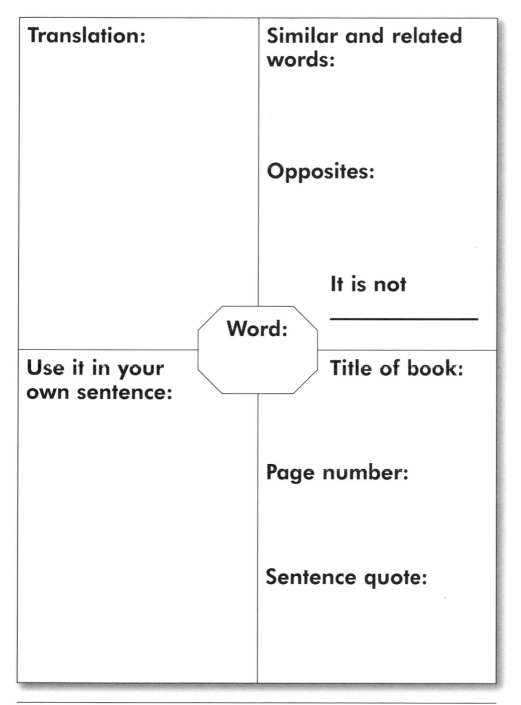

Translation:	Similar and related words:
	Opposites:
	It is not _____
Word:	
Use it in your own sentence:	Title of book:
	Page number:
	Sentence quote:

Bilingual Books for Compare and Contrast With a Food Theme

Eating (Swain, 1999c) (Arabic, Bengali, Chinese, Gujarati, Punjabi, Turkish, Urdu, Vietnamese) Stage 3. Themes: people, food, social studies. CLT: compare and contrast.

Fruits and Vegetables (Frutas y Vegetales) (Rosa-Mendoza, 2002) Stage 1. Theme: food. CLT: compare and contrast, visualizing.

Growing Vegetable Soup (A Sembrar Sopa de Verduras) (Ehlert, 1996b) Stage 2. Theme: food. CLT: realia, compare and contrast, LEA.

Let's Eat (Vamos A Comer) (Benjamin, 1992) Stage 1. Theme: food. CLT: compare and contrast.

The Milk Makers (Las Vacas Lecheras) (Gibbons, 1987) Stage 4. Themes: food, farms. CLT: compare and contrast.

Tell Me Traviesa, What Fruit Is That? (Dime Traviesa, ¿Qué Fruta es Ésa?) (Núñez, 2004) Stage 1. Theme: food. CLT: compare and contrast.

Tortillas and Lullabies /Tortillas y Cancioncitas) (Reiser, 1998) Stage 4. Themes: food, family. CLT: compare and contrast, recitation, reenactment.

Too Many Pears (English/Japanese bilingual edition) (French, 2007) Stage 2. Themes: humor, animals, food. CLT: compare and contrast.

Bilingual Books About Other Themes: Animals, Cats

Feathers for Lunch (Plumas Para Almorzar) (Ehlert, 1996a) Stage 4. Theme: cats. CLT: compare and contrast, reader's theater.

From Head to Toe (De Cabeza a Pies) (Carle, 2007a) Stage 2. Theme: animals. CLT: compare and contrast, chanting, TPR.

Hop, Jump (Salta y Brinca) (Walsh, 1996) Stage 3. Theme: animals. CLT: compare and contrast, reader's theater.

If You Give a Cat a Cupcake. (Si le Das un Pastelito a un Gato) (Numeroff, 2010) Stage 3. Themes: cats, food. CLT: compare and contrast.

Rooster/Gallo (Lujan & Monroy, 2004) Stage 1. Poem. Theme: animals. CLT: compare and contrast, reenactment, recitation.

That's Not My Kitten. (Este No Es Mi Gatito: Tiene Las Orejas Blandas) (Watt, 2001a) Stage 2. Theme: cats. CLT: chanting, compare and contrast.

Where Are You Going? To See My Friend! A Story of Friendship in English and Japanese (Iwamura & Carle, 2003) Stage 1 song. Theme: animals. CLT: chanting, singing, compare and contrast.

CHANTING WITH *SWEET POTATO PIE*

Sweet Potato Pie (Rockwell, 1996) is a classic early reading book with a catchy rhyme that supports fluency development. Its repetitive text reduces anxiety about errors. Chanting has no need of written text. However, certain types of texts are associated with specific activities:

- Sing-song patterned texts with rhythm and rhyme are used with choral recitation.
- Songbooks with lyrics, musical scores, and recordings are used with singing.
- Repetitive oral style texts are used for teaching oral intonation and stress patterns of English in *Jazz Chants* (Graham, 1978).
- Patterned sentences are used with cloze (Gunderson, 2009, p. 131).
- Poems and cumulative rhymes are used for recitation and poetry readings.

A number of informal assessments can be used to monitor fluency development, such as the dictation and writing scales described earlier in this book. In this lesson a writing task is used as an assessment.

Present and Model

1. Read *Sweet Potato Pie*. Reread the entire book while students clap or tap to its rhythm.

2. Reread it again, and have students gesture with each repetition of the title phrase, "sweet potato pie."

3. Reread and pause at the end of natural language phrases for students to complete the phrase by chiming in.

3. Have each student write a two-column list, on the left the words they already know and on the right the new ones to learn.

4. Have students make vocabulary cards for words in the right column.

Practice and Interact

1. Conduct a reenactment with the class. Make student teams. Have one team gesture the actions of a scene and the other team guess which scene it is.

2. Divide students into groups, and assign different lines to each. For example, have Group 1 say Line 1, Group 2 say Line 2, and so on.

3. List the characters, verbs, and foods in columns. Brainstorm and add these. Examples from the book are below.

Character Names	Verb Phrases	Foods
From the book: Everybody Grandma From our class: Our class Thalia	is baking is mixing is enjoying is cooking is eating	sweet potato pie sweet apple pie fresh pumpkin pie tangy lemon pie

4. Review the patterns in sentences with the students, such as

Everybody + 's + happy.

Grandma + 's baking + apple pie.

5. Have students judge whether a line is read with correct or incorrect intonation. When it is read correctly, they give it a thumbs up, and when it is read incorrectly, they give it a thumbs down.

6. Model substituting words from the character column into patterned sentences. Have students substitute. Model expanding sentences by combining and adding phrases. Have students do the same. Practice saying these aloud in unison.

7. Write the new sentences on the board. Call on students to read a randomly selected sentence. Call on others to identify the sentence by pointing to it.

Expand and Utilize

Make a Guessing Game

1. Have students draw pictures of people with foods, such as a hand spooning out a pumpkin, fingers pushing a button on a blender filled with berries, or people picking apples. Have them label items and actions.

2. On the bottom of each drawing, list the illustrator and give the drawing a number.

3. Post the drawings along a wall.

4. Assign each student a different picture to write a sentence about. Each student must read the sentence, and the class must guess the number

of the picture. Upper grade ELLs can expand this to using negative statements until the class guesses the picture, such as in the following examples:

> Lead student says, "It is not juice."
>
> The class confirms, "It is not Picture 2."
>
> Lead student says, "It is not red."
>
> The class confirms, "It is not Picture 3."

Lead student calls on individuals to continue guessing based on the remaining possibilities. The student who guesses correctly leads next.

Upper Grade ELLs

Upper grade ELLs can expand the activities of this lesson by incorporating language and information from the following books :

- *Peanut Butter and Jelly* (Westcott, 1992), poem.
- *The Pizza That We Made* (Holub, 2001).
- *What's Cookin'? A Happy Birthday Counting Book* (Coffelt, 2003), poetic text.

They can also use books with song lyrics for repetitive practice. The following are single-song books that are appropriate for upper grade ELLs:

- *Forever Young* (Dylan, 2008), familiar 1973 song by Bob Dylan.
- *Morning Has Broken* (Farjeon & Ladwig, 1996), song by Cat Stevens.
- *Pete the Cat: I Love My White Shoes* (Litwin, 2010), silly.
- *Pete the Cat: Rocking in My School Shoes* (Litwin, 2011), silly.
- *Sunshine on My Shoulders* (Canyon & Denver, 2003), John Denver song.
- *What a Wonderful World* (Weiss, Thiele, & Bryan, 1995), Louis Armstrong song.

Model-Based Writing

1. Write the following patterned phrases on the board and read them aloud:

> *What can you do with an apple pie? I can eat it. I can love it.*
>
> *What can't you do with an apple pie? I can't kick it.*

2. Have students brainstorm things they can/can't do with apple pie, and add these to a list on the board as in the example below. The third column also suggests other foods.

I can	I can't	Other Ideas (note number of syllables)
cut	kick	sweet potato pie, sweet potato
eat	wash	juicy cherry pie, cherries
love	write	creamy pumpkin pie, pumpkin
bake	stomp	sweet blueberry pie, blueberries
make	roll	tangy lemon pie, lemons
taste	squeeze	tasty apple pie, apples

3. Have students review the patterned phrases, practice them with a partner, and then write one of their own with their choice of words from the above columns. Then have partners chant their new phrases and repeat the my-oh-my pattern phrase from the book, as shown in the examples below:

Apple Pie Guided Interaction for Partners A and B		Lemon Pie Guided Interaction for Partners	
A:	What *can* you do with a tasty *apple pie?*	A:	What can you do with a *tangy lemon pie?*
B:	I can *eat it.*	B:	I can *cut it.*
A:	I can *taste it.*	A:	I can *bake it.*
A & B:	My oh my, what can I do with an *apple pie.*	A & B:	My oh my, a tangy *lemon pie.*
B:	What *can't* you do with an *apple pie?*	B:	What can't you do with a *lemon pie?*
A:	I can't *wash it.*	A:	I can't *kick it.*
B:	I can't either.	B:	I can't either.
A & B:	My oh my, you *can't* do that with *apple pie.*	A & B:	My oh my, you *can't* do that with *a lemon pie.*

4. Have students fill in the blanks on this guided interaction:

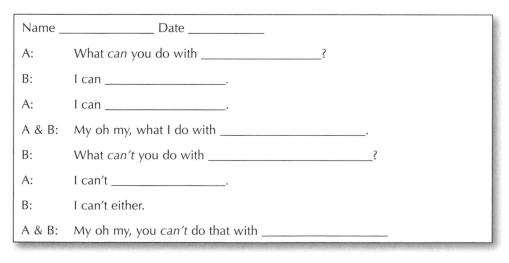

Name _____ Date _____	
A:	What *can* you do with _____?
B:	I can _____.
A:	I can _____.
A & B:	My oh my, what I do with _____.
B:	What *can't* you do with _____?
A:	I can't _____.
B:	I can't either.
A & B:	My oh my, you *can't* do that with _____

Assess With a Timed Writing

Conduct a timed writing of the story by having ELLs write this book's title on the top of a sheet of paper along with the date and the previously agreed upon allotted minutes. Tell the students to write as much and as accurately as they can about the book. Once the time is up, have them count the total number of words they wrote and their words per minute.

Books for Chanting or Singing About Food

Bread Is for Eating (Gershator, Gershator, & Shaw-Smith, 1998) Bilingual poetic text and song. Stage 4. Themes: food, people, social studies. CLT: reader's theater, singing, recitation.

Jump, Frog, Jump! (Kalan, 2002) Stage: Poem. Theme: food. CLT: chanting, reenactment.

Peanut Butter and Jelly (Westcott, 1992) Stage: Poem. Themes: humor, food. CLT: chanting.

The Pizza That We Made (Holub, 2001) Stage 3. Themes: food, people. CLT: chanting, TPR.

Ten Red Apples (Hutchins, 2000). Stage 1. Theme: food. CLT: chanting.

Sweet Potato Pie (Rockwell, 1996) Stage 2. Theme: food. CLT: chanting.

There Was an Old Lady (Holmes, 2009) Stage: Song. Theme: animals. CLT: chanting, singing.

What's Cookin'? (Coffelt, 2003) Stage 4. Themes: food, counting. CLT: LEA, chanting.

Books for Chanting or Singing About Other Themes: Animals, People

Forever Young (Dylan, 2008) Dylan's 1973 song. Stage: Song. Theme: people. CLT: singing.

Hats, Hats, Hats (Morris, 1993b) Stage 1. Theme: people, social studies. CLT: chanting.

Joseph Had a Little Overcoat (Taback, 1999) Stage: Song. Theme: people. CLT: singing.

Morning Has Broken (Farjeon & Ladwig, 1996) Stage: Song. Theme: CLT: singing.

No One Saw: Ordinary Things Through the Eyes of an Artist (Raczka, 2002) Stage 1. Theme: art. Older elementary. CLT: chanting.

One More River: A Noah's Ark Counting Book (Paley, 2002) Stage: Song. Themes: animals, numbers. CLT: singing.

Pete the Cat: I Love My White Shoes (Litwin, 2010) Stage: Song. Themes: animals, cats. CLT: singing.

Pete the Cat: Rocking in My School Shoes (Litwin, 2011). Stage 2. Song. Themes: animals, cats. CLT: singing.

Sunshine on My Shoulders (Canyon & Denver, 2003) Stage: Song. Theme: people. CLT: singing.

A Tree for Me (Van Laan, 2002) Stage 3. Poem. Theme: people. CLT: chanting.

Walking Through the Jungle (Blackstone & Harter, 2006) Stage 3. Theme: people. CLT: reenactment, chanting.

Way Up High in a Tall Green Tree (Peck, 2005) Stage 4. Poem. Theme: people. CLT: chanting.

What a Wonderful World (Weiss, Thiele, & Bryan, 1995) Stage: Song. Theme: concept. CLT: singing.

The Wheels on the School Bus (Moore, 2006) Stage: Song. Theme: people. CLT: singing.

Whoever You Are (Quienquiera Que Seas) (Fox, 2002) Stage: Poem. Theme: people. CLT: recitation, compare and contrast.

NOTES

1. See Yopp and Yopp (2001) for other examples.
2. For more examples, conduct an Internet image search of the term *wordmap*.

Unit About People With Four Strategies

The people theme includes more books for upper grade students than the other themes do, although all age groups can identify with content that revolves around families. The book-based activities selected here challenge English language learners (ELLs) to express needs, ideas, and opinions in writing. They include more academically oriented language strategies than others.

The comprehension strategy, visualizing, is used with *Cassie's Word Quilt* (Ringgold, 2004). This is a mixed-format concept book, with one text introducing words in semantically organized groups much like a picture dictionary. For expression, *Dear Daisy, Get Well Soon* (Smith, 2002) is used, because its text uses devices typical of notes and diaries. This lends itself to model-based writing. *Amelia's Fantastic Flight* (Bursik, 1994) contains graphics—maps that provide ELLs with opportunities to practice integrating verbal and visual information. Fluency is the focus of a recitation lesson using the poem *Honey, I Love* (Greenfield, 2002). The poem also lends itself to reenactment.

VISUALIZING WITH *CASSIE'S WORD QUILT*

Visual scaffolds are a staple of communicative language teaching (CLT) because they increase comprehension and opportunities for practicing new terms. ELLs can make personal and emotional connections to the main character of *Cassie's Word Quilt* (Ringgold, 2004). Its format serves as a scaffold for language-learning strategies because words are presented in sets of nine. Each new set of nine words appears in a three-by-three matrix of items based on a context, such as a bedroom. Additionally, each matrix has an accompanying scenario with a descriptive sentence. For example, there is a home matrix with nine words, a home scenario with labeled furniture items, and a descriptive sentence about how Cassie feels about the things in her home.

Vocabulary objectives for this lesson can be assessed by observing students during several explicit vocabulary activities. Teachers can develop a comprehension check or a vocabulary checklist to monitor vocabulary growth.

Prepare and Model

1. Conduct a picture walk to introduce the book.

2. Select a location in the book, and teach the nine words associated with it. Read the sentence. When appropriate, substitute or add one of the nine words into the sentence.

3. Have each student copy two or three different vocabulary words onto cards and illustrate them.

4. Once the cards are completed, shuffle them and redistribute them to pairs of students to review together. Pace the review of vocabulary, having them recall the words on just one card at first, progressively adding cards made by other students.

Practice and Interact

1. Read, comment on, and change the objects and sentences in each scenario. For example, use the sentence about Cassie's colorful clothes in the bedroom scene, and have students interact and manipulate the English in any of the following ways:

   a. Substitute one word for another, such as the noun *clothes* for another noun, or the modifier *colorful* for another modifier.

b. Replace the sentence statement with a question, such as "Does Cassie's bedroom have clothes?"

c. Challenge students to determine the veracity of a statement:

Her bedroom has colorful clothes. True.

Cassie's bedroom has cars. False.

2. Have each student draw a picture of Cassie and surround her with several items, such as her family, friends, places, and things. Place everyone's drawings on the board, where all students can see them. Select one, and begin describing it without telling students which one it is. Students must guess which picture is being described.

3. Have students make cards for the nouns and modifiers to play sorting, matching, and grouping card games, such as Go Fish. Here are a few suggestions for ways students can work with the vocabulary of this book:

a. Pair words that rhyme, such as *mother/father, brother/flower,* and *broom/bedroom.*

b. Distinguish between natural and human-made vocabulary words, such as *boy, man, brother, flower,* and *lamp* and *furniture.*

c. Make a second copy of each vocabulary card so there are pairs of cards for an appropriate number for the age group. The cards must be blank on the back. Scatter these on a table with the picture down. Have a student pick up one card and show it to the class, and have the next student pick up another card. The first student then asks the class, "Are they the same or different?" When two cards are picked that are the same, they are retired. The game finishes when all the cards are picked up.

d. Gather and sort the cards for nouns and modifiers, as shown in the columns below. Have students sort and combine them into phrases that make sense, such as *furry blanket, small bed,* and *small blanket,* but not *furry bed.*

Feel modifiers: *cold, hot, soft, hard, rough, smooth, furry* Size modifiers: *big, small, long, short, round, square* Color modifiers: *white, yellow, pink, red, blue, black*	Nouns: *lamp, girl, broom, bed, chest of drawers, fan, can, blanket, chair*

4. Designate a table to become mystery locations. Make cards with location names and object names, such as *NYC, Tar Beach, block, apartments,*

bedroom, school, and *home.* Select two location cards, and place these on opposite sides of the table. Give students object cards, and have them place these cards on either of the two sides of the table representing locations. Engage them in talking about their decisions, for example, "Do you think a bed goes with sand? A bed does not belong on the beach. It belongs here." Once students are familiar with the routine, create a scenario in which they do not know the location's designation. They are to guess the location as you place each item there. Keep placing items until students figure out the name of the location.

Utilize and Expand

Upper Grade ELLs

Using the list of books below, select and teach up to 20 words for more locations, small and large. Make word cards for each. On a large sheet of paper, draw a few concentric circles inside each other. Write *stars* outside the largest, and inside the smallest, write *me.* In the middle circles write *world, continents,* and *USA,* and have students place names of places, such as *NYC, Tar Beach,* and *bedroom,* in the appropriate circles.

Select a word card. Describe which circle it would go into using appropriate prepositions, such as *inside, outside,* and *next to.* Place it inside the appropriate circle. Allow students to pick cards and add parallel items to each circle.

- *The Red Book* (Lehman, 2004).
- *Re-Zoom* (Banyai, 1995).
- *Round Like a Ball* (Ernst, 2008).
- *Stars! Stars! Stars!* (Barner, 2002).
- *Zoom* (Banyai, 1995).

Have students take turns making a statement about each object, and have the class guess what the student is describing, for example, "It is outside the world; what is it?" The answer is *stars.*

Information Gap

Refer to the graphic on page 147 showing the three webs.

1. Each ELL is to label the squares in Web A: About Cassie. Have each individually write two or three examples of her family members, other people, things, or places in her life in each square. Then have student

partners share their webs with one another and discover the differences and similarities between their webs and their partner's.

3. Have each student complete Web B individually. Then have them fold their papers twice horizontally (as shown by the arrows), so that Web B is hidden but Webs A and C are visible. Each is to ask the other about the items in Web B. They are to record or take notes of their partner's Web B items on their own Web C.

4. Once this is done, the students compare their Web B with their partner's Web C and discover which items they understood correctly and which they did not.

Web A about Cassie:

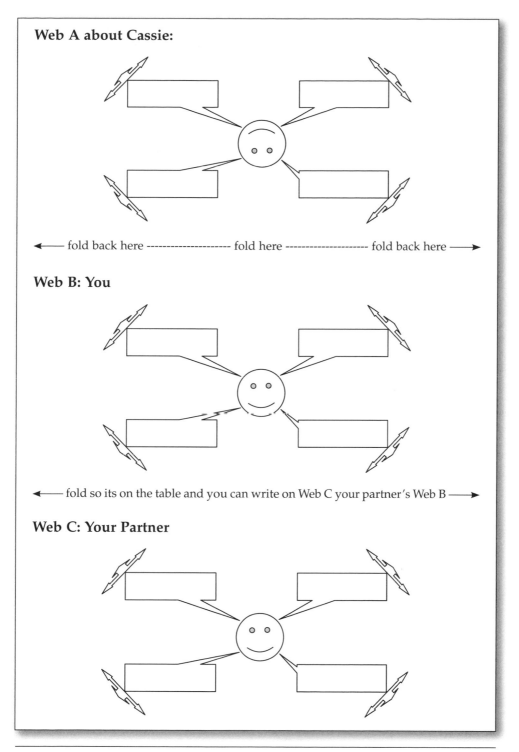

◄——— fold back here -------------------- fold here -------------------- fold back here ——►

Web B: You

◄——— fold so its on the table and you can write on Web C your partner's Web B ——►

Web C: Your Partner

Vocabulary Visuals[1]

Select a scene, and compare the nine words with comparable words associated with the students' homes. Teach them to identify things and attributes that are alike and that are different.

Cassie's bedroom had clothes. My bedroom has clothes, too. Our bedrooms are alike.

Have students work in pairs to create word banks based on semantic categories, such as those in the table below.

People	Objects	Comparisons	Locations
Cassie	Rug, pillow, bed, lamp, picture, blanket	Faster/slower	Bedroom
Mother		Softer/harder	New York City
Brother		Larger/smaller	Neighborhood
Sister		Different, alike, the same	Inside, Outside, next to

Students can use the word bank in this table to make a book of their own like *Cassie's Word Quilt*. A graphic organizer can help; the example below includes some sample filled-in items.

Plan Your Own Quilt Book

Title: Date: Number of pages: Locations:	1. Select favorite items from *Cassie's Word Quilt*.

	tall lamp		
	small rug	Cassie's Bedroom	

2. Select items from your own life.

tiny lamp		
wall to wall rug	Joe's Bedroom	
picture of pyramids		

Practice writing:

Cassie and I are _____.

Cassie lives in New York City. I live in _____.

Cassie has _____. I do not.

Cassie has _____. I do too.

I have a _____. Cassie does too.

My _____ is _____. Hers is _____.

Draft of my quilt book:

Assess

Develop scoring sheets for the types of vocabulary activities used. For example, the Plan Your Own Quilt Book organizer above can be scored for numbers of items included. The following are examples of possible assessment items for the word bank activity:

1. Able to combine two vocabulary column words to orally express one full sentence.

2. Able to combine three vocabulary column words to orally express two or more sentences.

3. Able to write sentences using vocabulary from the columns.

A comprehension check assessment can be developed by putting drawings of items from the book in rows on a page. Administer the assessment like a spelling test by asking students to look at the drawings in the first row and underline a particular one, and so on with subsequent rows.

Books for Visualizing

1 Hunter (Hutchins, 1982) Stage: Wordless. Themes: people, counting. CLT: visualizing, retelling.

31 Uses for a Mom (Ziefert, 2003) Stage 2. Picture dictionary of jobs. Themes: people, concept. CLT: visualizing.

A Is for Autumn (Maass, 2011) Stage 4. Themes: people, concept, seasons. CLT: visualizing.

The Arrival (Tan, 2007) Stage: Wordless. Themes: people, social studies. For upper grade ELLs. CLT: retelling.

Baby EyeLike: Triangle (Play Bac, 2008) Stage 1. Themes: people, concept. CLT: visualizing.

The Bag I'm Taking to Grandma's (Neitzel & Parker, 1998) Stage 3. Theme: people. CLT: visualizing.

The Eye Book (Seuss & Mathieu, 1999) Stage 2. Theme: people. CLT: visualizing.

Cassie's Word Quilt (Ringgold, 2004) Stage 3. Theme: people. CLT: visualizing.

Can You Find It?: Search and Discover More Than 150 Details in 19 Works of Art (Cressy, 2002) Stage 4. Themes: people, art. CLT: visualizing.

EyeLike: Numbers (Play Bac, 2007) Stage: Picture Dictionary. Themes: counting, concept. CLT: visualizing.

I Spy a Butterfly (Marzollo & Wick, 2006) Stage 4. Theme: concept. CLT: visualizing, guessing games.

Lebanon 1–2–3: A Counting Book in Three Languages, English—French—Arabic (Boueri & Dabaji, 2005) Stage 3. Theme: people. CLT: compare and contrast, guessing games, visualizing.

The Little Book of Not So: A Book of Opposites (Harper, 2005) Stage 2. Themes: concept. Picture dictionary of opposites. CLT: visualizing.

Me and My Family Tree (Sweeney, 2000) Stage 3. Themes: people, families. CLT: visualizing, LEA.

Mini Picture Dictionary (Turhan, 2003) Stage 1. Simplified picture dictionary. Bilingual Arabic, Chinese, Farsi, Kurdish, Russian, Somali, Turkish, Urdu. Theme: people. CLT: visualizing.

Milet Picture Dictionary (Turhan, 2005) Stage: Picture dictionary. Bilingual version available in many different bilingual versions. Theme: people. CLT: visualizing.

Night/Day: A Book of Eye-Catching Opposites (Tullet, 2005) Stage: Picture dictionary in cursive. Theme: concept. CLT: visualizing.

The Red Book (Lehman, 2004) Stage: Wordless. Themes: people, friendship. CLT: visualizing, retelling.

Round Like a Ball (Ernst, 2008) Stage 2. Themes: people, concept. CLT: guessing games, visualizing.

Shout! Shout It Out! (Fleming, 2011) Stage 2. Multitext. Picture dictionary (ABC, numbers, colors, animals, transportation). Theme: concept. CLT: visualizing, chanting.

Stars! Stars! Stars! (Barner, 2002) Stage 4. Multitext. Upper Grade ELLs. Theme: science. CLT: recitation, compare and contrast, visualizing.

NOTES

1. For other examples of these types of activities, see *Teaching Thinking Skills With Picture Books* (Polette, 2007) and *Literature-Based Reading Activities* (Yopp & Yopp, 2006).

MODEL-BASED WRITING WITH *DEAR DAISY, GET WELL SOON*

Written models are ubiquitous in CLT with beginners because these create an atmosphere of success. ELLs use these models as stepping-stones until they are able to successfully engage in more creative expression. *Dear Daisy, Get Well Soon* (Smith, 2000) contains examples of the language used in a letter and a diary. ELLs can use it as a template for a personalized version. Since its illustrations appeal to younger ELLs, there are other suggestions in the lesson for upper grade ELLs.

Writing objectives can be assessed using the previously described writing scale. In addition, a checklist of items can be developed to evaluate the dialogue journal entry included in this lesson. Teachers can check dialogue journal entries at different intervals of time, for example, every four weeks, and make anecdotal notes of skill development.

Present and Model

1. List the days of the week on the board in a column. Leave second and third columns blank.

2. Read *Dear Daisy, Get Well Soon* and conduct a picture walk through it. Focus attention on literary devices, such as *Dear* and *Sincerely*.

3. On the board, add verbs from the book to the second column and gifts or locations to the third. The idea is to use the options in each column to produce new sentences.

   Sunday—made—cookies.

   Monday—went—to school.

4. Reread the book, stopping to add items to the chart and to have ELLs enact scenes created with combinations from the three columns.

5. If it is an appropriate challenge, guide ELLs to report what is said:

   She said that she . . .

Day	Did	Location or Gifts
Sunday,	stayed	no school
Monday,	went	at home
today, tomorrow, yesterday	picked	apples
Tuesday,	blew up	books
	made	card
	sent	balloons

Practice and Interact

1. Reread the book, but read the day, number, or gift wrong, and let students correct you.

2. If appropriate for your students' level of English language proficiency (ELP), have them report as follows:

It says that he. . . .

The book shows that. . . .

3. Place the names of all the students in a bucket. Give students each a blank card and markers. Have them pick a name from the bucket and imagine giving that person a gift by drawing the gift or writing what it is on the blank card. Have them share this with the class as follows:

Student A: "Today, I made a picture for Jessica."

Class responds together: "She said that she made a picture for Jessica."

Jessica: "Thanks."

4. Make a three-column chart, but add the dates in the second column, and combine the verb with its object in the third column. Have students mix and match from the columns to make a sentence, for example, "Today, March 3rd, I made a card." Each student is to read her or his sentence to the class. Classmates are to listen and identify the items in the columns.

Day	Date	Actions Past Tense
Today, Tomorrow, Yesterday	January 1st	made a card
Monday, Tuesday,	February 2nd	sent balloons
Last night	March 3rd	picked apples
Last year		picked a book

5. Role-play a visit to a far-away friend, and have students make a book about the experience. You may need to preview and guide the book's content, using phrases such as *who went, who invited, where is it, when did you go,* and *what did you do?* Have students complete the following:

- Write a title and make a cover page.
- Include an introductory sentence on the first page and a concluding one at the end.
- Include a map to locate a setting.
- Illustrate people involved.
- Include a calendar with the dates marked.

Utilize and Expand

Expand to Other Books

1. Select a few books with distinct literary devices, such as letters, journals, and art projects. Allow students to sort them into piles by text styles.

2. Select a book about art projects by Ed Emberley, such as one of the following:

- *Ed Emberley's Big Green Drawing Book* or *Ed Emberley's Big Purple Drawing Book*
- *Ed Emberley's Drawing Book of Trucks*, or *Ed Emberley's Drawing Book of Animals*
- *Ed Emberley's Great Thumbprint Drawing Book*
- *Ed Emberley's Picture Pie*

   a. Teach four illustrations, one at a time. Have ELLs use them to make greeting cards to send to friends and family.

   b. Give each student a blank sheet divided into four sections. Begin describing the procedure for one illustration. They are to complete it in one section of their paper. Have them check each other's interpretations.

   c. Select a student to give directions for another illustration for a second section of the paper. Continue until all four have been practiced.

   d. Select another set of four illustrations to master, and repeat the activity.

Technology

One online resource for teaching writing is a letter generator; see http://www.readwritethink.org/files/resources/interactives/letter_generator.

Assess With Dialogue Journals

Dialogue journals create opportunities for teachers to write letters back and forth with students. The teacher's response repeats the student's ideas, provides models for students to incorporate into their subsequent letters on the subject, expands upon their ideas, and always asks them a question.

The student's letter must adhere to guidelines. I suggest that you set a required minimum amount of time or number lines. The following is an example of an entry with a maximum amount of scaffolds; the template below can be modified to the ELP level of the students:

Monday, August 20th

Dear Student,

I liked the *Dear Daisy* book.

Did you like it? Yes or No

My favorite quote is "On Saturday I got a note that said, 'Please come over.'"

I also think crayons are a good gift because I like to draw. Do you?

Sincerely,

Your Teacher

Month _____ Date _____ Year _____

Dear _____,

I like _____

My favorite _____. What is your _____?

My _____ _____

Sincerely,

Your student, _____

To use the dialogue journal for assessment, select an entry written four to eight weeks earlier. Reread the book that prompted that entry, and have the student write another entry. Compare the two entries, noting the student's progress.

Books With Letters, Notes, or Diaries for Model-Based Writing

Dear Daisy, Get Well Soon (Smith, 2000) Stage 1. Theme: people. CLT: model-based writing.

Dear Mr. Blueberry (James, 1996) Stage 4. Appropriate for middle and high school. Themes: people, animals. CLT: model-based writing.

Draw Me a Star (Carle, 1992) Stage 1. End page contains a letter. Theme: art. CLT: model-based writing.

The Earth Book (Parr, 2010) Stage 3. Theme: poem. CLT: model-based writing.

First Year Letters (Danneberg, 2003) Stage 4. Theme: people. CLT: model-based writing.

I Wanna Iguana (Orloff, 2004) Stage 4. Themes: humor, family. CLT: model-based writing.

If You'll Be My Valentine (Rylant, 2005) Stage: Poems. Theme: people. CLT: model-based writing.

The Journey of Oliver K. Woodman (Pattison, 2003) Map. Stage: Multistage. Themes: social studies, people. CLT: model-based writing, retelling, graphics.

The Night Before Valentine's Day (Wing, 2000) Stage 3. Theme: friendship. CLT: model-based writing, recitation.

Send It! (Carter, 2003) Stage 1. Theme: people. CLT: TPR, model-based writing—days of the week.

Snowball (Crews, 1997) Stage 3. Theme: weather. CLT: model-based writing—days of the week.

When the Moon Is Full: A Lunar Year (Pollock, 2001) Stage: Multistage. Theme: poem. CLT: recitation, compare and contrast, model-based writing—months of the year.

Written Anything Good Lately? (Allen, Lindaman, & Enright, 2006) Stage 4. Theme: people. CLT: model-based writing, compare and contrast.

Books for Model-Based Writing Books on Other Themes: Animals

Click, Clack, Moo: Cows That Type (Cronin, 2000) Stage 4. Theme: animals. CLT: model-based writing.

Diary of a Spider (Cronin, 2005) Stage 4. Theme: animals. CLT: model-based writing.

Diary of a Wombat (French, 2003) Stage 4. Theme: animals. CLT: model-based writing.

Sleepy Bear (Dabcovich, 1993) Stage 1. Theme: animals. CLT: model-based writing—seasons.

Today Is Monday. (Carle, 1987b) Stage 1. Themes: food, animals. CLT: model-based writing—days of week.

GRAPHIC ORGANIZERS WITH
AMELIA'S FANTASTIC FLIGHT

Graphic organizers are an essential tool for teaching academic language. Graphic representations help ELLs see connections among ideas and thus better understand comparable linguistic devices (Graney, 1992). For example, a time line clarifies the meaning of sequential markers, a Venn diagram of comparatives, and maps of prepositions of location. In *Amelia's Fantastic Flight* (Bursik, 1994), small maps are included in each leg of the protagonist's journey. The map on the end page summarizes the entire trip.

Teachers can observe students' use of maps and students' ability to transfer information back and forth from a graphic to a written essay before and after book-based activities. A checklist is provided and should be adapted to assess students' ability to transfer information from graphic to verbal summaries and vice versa.

Present and Model

1. Conduct a picture walk through the book, and model ways to talk about the evidence provided by maps, pictures, and text. Teach students to answer the question *How do you know?* with patterned full sentences, such as the following:

> *What is her name? How do you know? I can read it in the title.*
>
> *Where does she go? How do you know? I can see it on the map.*
>
> *What is it like there? How do you know? I can see a picture.*
>
> *How did she travel? How do you know? It is on this page.*

2. Make a graphic organizer with the distinct scenes of the story. Model filling in the information by consulting the pictures, maps, and text.

Practice and Interact

1. Have students select their favorite page and talk about it. Prompt with the following types of questions, as needed:

> *What is your favorite part? Where is it? What is it like? How do you know?*

2. Have students ask each other these types of questions.

3. Cut apart the scenes in the graphic organizer you made and scramble them. Have students work in groups to put them in sequential order.

4. Use the graphic organizer on page 158 for students to make notes and map their favorite scene.

Amelia's Fantastic Flight: My Favorite Scene

She made a stop before _____ on page _____

and after _____ on page _____.

It was _____.

She saw a _____.

She liked _____.

I like _____.

Map of Location

Illustration of Location

Utilize and Expand

Expand

Modify the graphic organizer to use with an imaginary extra stop in Amelia's trip, and have students fill in the details about the new destination. The destination may be one that is familiar to all, such as their school, or it may be personal, such as another country where a relative lives.

Extra Episodes	
She made this extra stop before page _____ and after page _____.	
She stopped in _____.	
She saw _____.	
It was _____.	
She liked _____.	
Map of Location	Illustration of Location

Role-Play

Make a labeled map with three locations of importance to students. Have students illustrate key items associated with each location. Review with them ways to describe information about a place, invite a visitor, accept an invitation, buy something, or bring a gift to show others who did not go. Assign a student to represent each location. The student is to role-play inviting the class to visit. The class is to role-play accepting. Talk through visiting each location.

Upper Grade ELLs

Have students hunt for maps in other books. The following have a variety of types of maps:

- *Follow the Line Around the World* (Ljungkvist, 2008).
- *How to Make an Apple Pie and See the World* (Priceman, 1996).
- *The Secret Birthday Message* (Carle, 1986).

For each map, review the types of information and ways to represent it. Compare and contrast one of these to the maps in the book about Amelia.

Have students write short descriptions of their favorite place in the world and make a map showing its location.

Assess

Develop a checklist to score either of the following tasks:

1. Provide ELLs with a blank map. Read the title page and at least three pages of the book. Have students mark the locations you are reading about on their maps as you read. A checklist of five points can be used to score their maps. The following are five suggested items:

__ Title

__ Shows continents and oceans

__ Labels three locations

__ Has a legend

__ Shows the beginning, middle, and end of Amelia's journey

2. Provide ELLs with the graphic organizer on page 161 to fill in.

Book Title:

Page number: _____

Copy here the written text on this page: _____

Underline the location in the above sentence.

Think of a word describing the location and write it: _____

Where did Amelia go before? _____

Describe it in one word: _____

Where did she go after? _____

Describe it: _____

Where would you like to go? _____

What would you do? _____

BELOW:

Draw a world map.

Locate your home on it.

Locate a place from *Amelia's Fantastic Journey.*

Show the path of the journey.

Include a legend.

Books for Graphic Organizers

A Giraffe Goes to Paris (Holmes & Harris, 2010) Stage 4—Intermediate. Appropriate for high school. Theme: CLT: retelling, graphics, visualizing.

Abuelita Fue al Mercado / My Granny Went to Market (Blackstone, 2007) Stage 4. Themes: family, map. CLT: realia, graphics, visualizing.

Amelia's Fantastic Flight (Bursik, 1994) Stage 2. Themes: people, social studies, map. CLT: graphics.

Buster (Fleming, 2008) Stage 4. Theme: friendship, map. CLT: graphics.

Follow the Line Around the World (Ljungkvist, 2008) Stage 4. Appropriate for high school. Theme: social studies. CLT: visualizing, graphics.

Follow the Line Through the House (Ljungkvist, 2007) Stage 4. Appropriate for high school. Theme: concept. CLT: visualizing, guessing games, graphics.

The Fossil Girl: Mary Anning's Dinosaur Discovery (Brighton, 1999) Stage 4. Appropriate for high school. Themes: people, history. CLT: visualizing, reader's theater.

Me on the Map (Sweeney, 1996) Stage 3. Theme: people. CLT: graphics.

The Secret Birthday Message (Carle, 1986) Stage 2. Theme: people. CLT: reenactment, graphics.

Walking Through the Jungle (Harter & Blackstone, 2004) Stage 2. Themes: social studies, people. CLT reenactment, graphics.

Wow! America! (Neubecker, 2006) Stage 2. Themes: social studies, map. CLT: graphics.

You and Me Together: Moms, Dads, and Kids Around the World (Kerley, 2010) Stage 1. Appropriate for high school. Themes: family, social studies, map. CLT: compare and contrast, recitation, graphics.

Young Christopher Columbus: Discoverer of New Worlds (Carpenter, 1996) Stage 4. Appropriate for high school. Theme: social studies. CLT: graphics.

RECITATION WITH *HONEY, I LOVE*

Recitation is an ideal way to respond to a single-poem picture book and develop fluency. The poem *Honey, I Love* (Greenfield, 2002) lends itself to recitation. Rehearsing with a group helps improve their intonation, pronunciation, facial expressions, and interpretation. This poem also lends itself to dramatic reenactment, because each stanza represents a different scene. Have small groups of students each practice a different stanza. Afterward, the groups can cooperate to ensure smooth transitions between stanzas when they dramatize the entire poem. Once a poem with patterned sentences becomes familiar, students can expand it by rewriting it with substituted vocabulary.

Several informal assessments can be used to monitor objectives related to poetry recitation. The retelling scale can be modified to accommodate the nuances of the poetry recital. Written fluency can be checked with pre and post timed writings about the poem's theme.

Present and Model

1. Review the pictures and stanzas while focusing ELLs' attention on meanings of key words.

2. Read the poem page by page, and focus on comprehension by having students reenact each scene.

3. Reread it and draw students' attention to poetic devices, such as any of the following:
   - Repetition of the phrase, "Honey, I love. . . ."
   - Patterned verses
   - Point of view
   - Descriptive words
   - Rhyming words, such as *south/mouth, walks/talks, cool/pool,* and *eat/meet*

Practice and Interact

1. Divide the poem into stanzas.

2. Assign a small group of students to review each stanza.

3. Have the groups rehearse, interpret with gestures, and practice appropriate intonation for reciting their stanzas.

4. Bring the class together to rehearse and cooperatively work on the transitions between the stanzas.

5. Have the class perform the entire poem.

6. Remix students into new groups. Assign different stanzas to these new groups and tell them to rehearse their new stanzas together.

Expand and Utilize

1. With the students, list key and interesting words in the poem. Engage them in making word cards for each and sorting them, for example, by word type, as in the following examples:

- Verbs: *spray, make, kiss, ride, play, eat,* and *laugh*
- Nouns for family members: *mama, grandpa, grandma, aunt, cousin, sister*
- Modifiers: *laughing, crowded, crispy, wet, sticky, tan*

2. Have them add other associated words, saying, for example, "The poem uses *tan;* what other colors do you know? Let's add these to our list."

3. Have each student select two associated words from the list and explain how their words are associated. For example, a student might select *tan* and *red* and say they are colors, or *crispy* and *wet* and say they can be felt.

4. With the students, list the lines in the poem. Engage the students in finding patterns. Have each student rewrite one line by adding a new modifier or personalized information. Students can use the form in the box on page 165 for this activity.

Your name:

Poem Title:

Author:

1. Line of the poem:

Color words I selected to add:

New line:

2. Another line of the poem:

Feel words I selected to add:

New line:

Have students practice reading their new lines to a partner. When they are ready, have them read their lines to the class. Give each student one suggestion for improving his or her delivery.

Expand to Other Books With Four Corners Jigsaw

1. Divide the class into four groups by assigning each student a number from and one to four. Assign each number a particular poem. The following are some suggested picture books with poems:

- *Cool Drink of Water* (Kerley, 2002).
- *Coretta Scott* (Shange, 2009).
- *Guyku: A Year of Haiku for Boys* (Raczka, 2010).
- *Imagine a Day* (Thomson, 2005).
- *Knoxville, Tennessee* (Giovanni, 1994).
- *My America* (Gilchrist, 2007).
- *My Many Colored Days* (Seuss 1998).
- *My People* (Hughes, 2009a).
- *The Negro Speaks of Rivers* (Hughes, 2009b).
- *Owl Moon* (Yolen & Schoenherr, 1987).
- *Peace* (Kerley 2007).
- *You and Me Together: Moms, Dads, and Kids Around the World* (Kerley, 2010).

2. Have students of each group practice for a performance of their poem.

3. Bring the class together, and have each group of students perform their poem.

4. Have students select a partner and another poem. Conduct a poetry recital.

Assess With an Oral Rubric

As was done in the appendix with the reader's theater lesson, develop an oral rubric to reflect clear objectives of the poetry recital.

Assess With Timed Writing

Conduct a timed writing before reading the book, using the two steps below. After completing the lesson and the substitution and expansion exercises, conduct another timed writing.

1. Have ELLs write the title of the book, the date, and the amount of allotted time in minutes on a sheet of paper. Clarify with them that they are to write as much as they can accurately in the allotted time.

2. Start the clock. Stop at the allotted time, count the words the students have written, and figure their words per minute.

Poetry Books With a People Theme

Coretta Scott (Shange, 2009) Stage 4 Poem. Upper grade ELLs. Themes: people, social studies. CLT: recitation.

Cool Drink of Water (Kerley, 2002) Stage 2. Appropriate for all ages. Stage: Multistage. Themes: people, social studies, map. CLT: recitation, compare and contrast.

Dance (Jones, 1998) Stage 2. Appropriate for all ages. Theme: people. CLT: recitation, reenactment.

Daughter, Have I Told You? (Coyne, 1998) Stage: Poem. Theme: people. CLT: recitation, chanting.

The Desert Is My Mother / El Desierto es Mi Madre (Mora, 1994) Poem. Theme: people. Stage 3. Spanish/English. CLT: recitation.

The Earth and I (Asch, 1994) Stage: Poem. Theme: science. CLT: recitation.

The Earth is Good: A Chant in Praise of Nature (DeMunn, 1999) Stage 1. Poem. Themes: people, nature. CLT: recitation.

Follow Me (Tusa, 2011) Stage 2 Poem. Appropriate for all ages. Theme: nature. CLT: recitation, reenactment.

Guyku: A Year of Haiku for Boys (Raczka, 2010) Six humorous Stage 3 haiku per each season. Upper grade ELLs. See samples and activities in http://www.guykuhaiku.com. Theme: language arts. CLT: recitation.

Imagine a Day (Thomson, 2005) Stage 4 poem. Theme: people. Upper grade ELLs. CLT: recitation, model-based writing.

In the Fiddle Is a Song (Bernheard, 2006) Stage: Poem. Theme: nature. CLT: recitation.

Kente Colors (Chocolte, 1996) Stage 1. Capital letter fonts. Theme: people. CLT: recitation.

Knoxville, Tennessee (Giovanni, 1994) Stage 2. Theme: families. CLT: recitation.

My America (Gilchrist, 2007) Stage 2. Themes: people, social studies. CLT: recitation.

My Many Colored Days (Seuss, 1998) Stage: Poem. Interesting to all age groups. Theme: people. CLT: recitation.

My People (Hughes, 2009a) Stage 1. Poem. Interesting to all age groups. Theme: people. CLT: recitation.

The Negro Speaks of Rivers (Hughes, 2009b). Stage 4. Upper grade ELLs. Themes: social studies, language arts. CLT: recitation.

One Love (Marley, 2011) Stage 1 Song. Themes: people, families. CLT: recitation, singing.

Owl Moon (Yolen & Schoenherr, 1987) Stage 4. Poem. Upper grade ELLs. Theme: people. CLT: recitation.

Peace (Kerley, 2007) Stage 2–multistage. Poem. Upper grade ELLs. Theme: people. CLT: recitation, compare and contrast.

Say Hello (Foreman & Foreman, 2008) Stage 2. Theme: friendship. CLT: recitation.

Songs for the Seasons (Highwater, 1995) Multistage poems. Themes: science, people. CLT: recitation, compare and contrast.

Visiting Langston (Perdomo, 2002) Stage 2. Theme: people. CLT: recitation.

When I First Came to This Land (Ziefert & Brand, 2007) Stage: Poem. Theme: people. CLT: recitation, retelling.

You and Me Together: Moms, Dads, and Kids Around the World (Kerley, 2010) Stage 2–multistage. Theme: people. CLT: recitation, compare and contrast.

The World Turns Round and Round (Weiss, 2002) Stage 4. Themes: people, social studies, map. CLT: recitation, compare and contrast.

Children's Book References and Resources

Adams, P. (2003). *There was an old lady who swallowed a fly* (Classic Books With Holes). Swindon, UK: Child's Play.

Alakija, P. (2002). *Catch that goat!* Cambridge, MA: Barefoot Books.

Aliki. (2009). *Quiet in the garden* New York, NY: Greenwillow Books.

Allen, S., Lindaman, J., &. Enright, V. (2006). *Written anything good lately?* Minneapolis, MN: Millbrook Press.

Allen, J. (2000a). *Are you a butterfly?* New York, NY: Kingfisher.

Allen, J. (2000b). *Are you a ladybug?* New York, NY: Kingfisher.

Allen, J. (2002). *Are you a grasshopper?* New York, NY: Kingfisher.

Allen, P. (1996). *Who sank the boat?* New York, NY: Puffin.

Anthony, J., & Arbo, C. (1997). *The dandelion seed.* Nevada City, CA: Dawn.

Argueta, J. (2009). *Sopa de frijoles/Bean soup.* Berkeley, CA: Groundwood.

Aruego, J. (1988). *Look what I can do.* New York, NY: Aladdin.

Asch, F. (1994). *The earth and I.* Orlando, FL: Harcourt Brace.

Aston, D. (2007). *A seed is sleepy.* San Francisco, CA: Chronicle Books.

Ayres, K. (2007). *Up, down, and around.* Cambridge, MA: Candlewick Press.

Banyai, I. (1995). *Re-Zoom.* New York, NY: Puffin.

Banyai, I. (1995). *Zoom.* New York: NY: Puffin.

Barner, B. (1999). *Bugs! bugs! bugs!* San Francisco, CA: Chronicle Books.

Barner, B. (2002). *Stars! stars! stars!* San Francisco, CA: Chronicle Books.

Barton, B. (1982). *Airport.* New York, NY: HarperCollins.

Barton, B. (1998). *Airplanes* (1st ed.). New York, NY: HarperFestival.

Barton, B. (2001). *My car* (1st ed.). New York, NY: Greenwillow Books.

Benjamin, A. (1992). *Let's eat / Vamos a comer.* (Chubby Little Simon ed.). New York, NY: Little Simon.

Berger, M. (2008). *Butterflies and caterpillars* (Scholastic true or false). New York, NY: Scholastic.

Bernheard, D. (2006). *In the fiddle is a song: A lift-the-flap book of hidden potential.* San Francisco, CA: Chronicle Books.

Blackstone, S. (2005). *My granny went to market.* Cambridge, MA: Barefoot.

Blackstone, S. (2007). *Abuelita fue al Mercado/My granny went to market*. Cambridge, MA: Barefoot.

Blackstone, S., & Harter, D. (2003). *Where's the cat?* (Board Book ed.). Cambridge, MA: Barefoot.

Blackstone, S., & Mockford, C. (2000). *Cleo the cat*. Cambridge, MA: Barefoot.

Bogacki, T. (1997). *Cat and mouse in the rain*. New York, NY: Farrar, Straus and Giroux.

Boueri, M., & Dabaji, M. T. (2005). *Lebanon 1–2-3: A counting book in three languages, English—French—Arabic*. Exeter, NH: Publishing Works.

Braun, S. (2009). *Meow and the big box*. London, UK: Boxer.

Bridwell, N. (2000). *Clifford makes a friend*. New York, NY: Cartwheel Books, Scholastic.

Brighton, C. (1999). *The fossil girl: Mary Anning's dinosaur discovery*. Brookfield, CT: Millbrook Press.

Brimner, L. D. (2000). *Cat on wheels*. Honesdale, PA: Boyds Mills Press.

Brown, M. W. (1999). *I like bugs*. New York, NY: Golden Books, Random House Books for Young Readers.

Brown, M. W. (2003). *Sneakers, the seaside cat*. New York, NY: HarperCollins.

Brown, R. (2000). *Holly: The true story of a cat* (1st American ed.). New York, NY: Henry Holt.

Brown, R. (2001a). *Diez semillas / Ten seeds*. New York, NY: Alfred A. Knopf.

Brown, R. (2001b). *Ten seeds*. New York, NY: Alfred A. Knopf.

Browne, A. (2001). *My dad* (1st American ed.). New York, NY: Farrar, Straus and Giroux.

Browne, A. (2009). *My mom* (1st American ed.). New York, NY: Farrar, Straus and Giroux.

Bruel, N. (2005). *Bad kitty*. New York, NY: Macmillan.

Bull, J. (2002). *The cooking book: 50 mouthwatering meals and sensational snacks*. New York: NY: DK Children.

Bryan, A. (2007). *Let it shine: Three favorite spirituals*. New York, NY: Atheneum Books for Young Readers.

Bunting, E. (1994). *Flower garden/Jardin de flores*. New York, NY: Scholastic.

Bunting, E. (1999). *Butterfly house*. New York, NY: Scholastic.

Bunting, E. (2000). *Flower garden*. Orlando, FL: Harcourt.

Bunting, E., & Cocca-Leffler, M. (2005). *My backpack*. Honesdale, PA: Boyds Mills.

Bursik, R. (1994). *Amelia's fantastic flight* (1st ed.). New York, NY: Henry Holt.

Canizares, S. (1998). *Butterfly*. New York, NY: Scholastic.

Canizares, S. (2003). *Butterfly/Mariposa*. New York, NY: Scholastic.

Canizares, S., & Chanko, P. (2003). *What do insects do?/Que hacen los insectos?* New York, NY: Scholastic.

Canizares, S., & Reid, M. (1998). *What is an insect?* New York, NY: Scholastic.

Canizares, S., & Reid, M. (2003). *Where do insects live?/Donde viven los insectos?* New York, NY: Scholastic.

Canyon, C., & Denver, J. (2003). *Sunshine on my shoulders* (1st ed.). Nevada City, CA: Dawn.

Caple, K. (2000). *Well done, Worm!* Cambridge, MA: Candlewick Press.

Caple, K. (2001). *Wow, it's worm*. Cambridge, MA: Candlewick Press.

Caple, K. (2005). *Termite trouble*. Cambridge, MA: Candlewick Press.

Carle, E. (1986). *The secret birthday message*. New York, NY: HarperCollins.

Carle, E. (1987a). *Have you seen my cat?* New York, NY: Aladdin.

Carle, E. (1987b). *Today is Monday.* New York, NY: Philomel Books.

Carle, E. (1990). *Pancakes, pancakes!* New York, NY: Simon & Schuster Books for Young Readers.

Carle, E. (1992). *Draw me a star.* New York, NY: Philomel Books.

Carle, E. (2003). *From head to toe.* New York, NY: Harper Collins.

Carle, E. (2007a). *From head to toe / De cabeza a pies.* New York, NY: HarperFestival.

Carle, E. (2007b). *My very first book of food* (Board Book ed.). New York, NY: Philomel.

Carle, E. (2009). *The very hungry caterpillar pop-up book.* New York, NY: Philomel Books.

Carlstrom, N. W. (1991). *Goodbye, geese.* New York, NY: Philomel.

Carpenter, E. (1996). *Young Christopher Columbus: Discoverer of new worlds.* Mahwah NJ: Troll Communications.

Carter, D. (1995). *Feely bugs: To touch and feel* (Bugs in a Box series). New York, NY: Little Simon.

Carter, D. (2003). *Send it!* Brookfield, CT: Roaring Brook Press.

Carter, D. (2006). *How many bugs in a box? A pop-up counting book.* New York, NY: Little Simon.

Child, L. (2000). *I will not ever never eat a tomato.* Cambridge, MA: Candlewick Press.

Chocolte, D. (1996). *Kente colors* New York, NY: Walker.

Coffelt, N. (2003). *What's cookin'?: A happy birthday counting book.* San Francisco, CA: Chronicle Books.

Cole, H. (1995). *Jack's garden.* New York, NY: Greenwillow Books.

Collicutt, P. (2000). *This plane* (1st ed.). New York, NY: Farrar, Straus and Giroux.

Collicutt, P. (2001). *This boat* (1st ed.). New York, NY: Farrar, Straus and Giroux.

Collicutt, P. (2002). *This car* (1st ed.). New York, NY: Farrar, Straus and Giroux.

Cook, M. (2009). *Our children can soar: A celebration of Rosa, Barack, and the pioneers of change.* New York, NY: Bloomsbury.

Coyne, R. (1998). *Daughter, have I told you?* (1st ed.). New York, NY: Henry Holt.

Cressy, J. (2002). *Can You Find It? Search and Discover More Than 150 Details in 19 Works of Art.* New York, NY: Harry N. Abrams.

Crews, D. (1985). *Bicycle race* (1st ed.). New York, NY: Greenwillow Books.

Crews, D. (1986). *Flying.* New York, NY: Greenwillow Books.

Crews, D. (1987). *Harbor.* New York, NY: Greenwillow Books.

Crews, D. (1991). *Truck.* New York, NY: Greenwillow Books.

Crews, D. (1993). *School bus.* New York, NY: Greenwillow Books.

Crews, D. (1995a). *Sail away* (1st ed.). New York, NY: Greenwillow Books.

Crews, D. (1995b) *Ten black dots* (board book ed.). New York, NY: Greenwillow Books.

Crews, N. (1997). *Snowball.* New York, NY: Greenwillow Books.

Cronin, D. (2000). *Click, clack, moo: Cows that type.* New York, NY: Simon & Schuster Books for Young Readers.

Cronin, D. (2005). *Diary of a spider.* New York, NY: Joanna Cotler Books.

Cronin, D. (2007). *Diary of a fly.* New York, NY: Joanna Cotler Books.

Cronin, D., & Menchin, S. (2009). *Stretch* (1st ed.). New York, NY: Atheneum Books for Young Readers.

Crozon, A. (2000). *I have wheels, what am I?* (bilingual ed.) London, UK: Milet Publishing.

Dabcovich, L. (1993). *Sleepy bear.* New York, NY: Dutton.

Danneberg, J. (2003). *First year letters.* Watertown, MA: Charlesbridge. .

Davis, K. (2001). *Who hops?* New York, NY: Harcourt.

Davis, K. (2004). *Who hoots?* San Diego, CA: Harcourt.

Day, A. (1994). *Carl makes a scrapbook.* New York: Simon & Schuster.

Day, A. (1998). *Follow Carl.* New York, NY: Simon & Schuster.

De Paola, T. (1990). *Pancakes for breakfast.* Orlando, FL: Voyager.

De Vicq de Cumptich, R. (2000). *Bembo's zoo: An animal ABC book.* New York, NY: Henry Holt.

Demarest, C., & Mayer, B. (2008). *All aboard! A traveling alphabet.* New York, NY: Margaret K. McElderry.

DeMunn, M. (1999). *The earth is good: A chant in praise of nature.* New York, NY: Scholastic.

DePalma, M. (2005). *The grand old tree.* New York, NY: Arthur A. Levine Books.

DK Publishing. (2010). *Garden friends* (DK readers pre-level 1). New York, NY: DK.

Dodd, E. (2009). *I don't want a cool cat!* (1st ed.). New York, NY: Little, Brown Books for Young Readers.

Dodd, E. (2011). *I love bugs!* New York, NY: Holiday House.

Downing, J. (2006). *Today is Monday in Louisiana.* Gretna, LA: Pelican.

Doyle, M. (2004). *Storm cats.* New York, NY: Pocket Children's Books.

Dussling, J. (1999). *Bugs! bugs! bugs! (Eyewitness Readers Level 2)* London, UK; New York, NY: DK Children.

Dylan, B. (2008). *Forever young.* New York, NY: Atheneum Books for Young Readers.

Ehlert, L. (1988). *Planting a rainbow.* Orlando, FL: Voyager.

Ehlert, L. (1989a). *Color zoo.* New York, NY: Lippincott.

Ehlert, L. (1989b). *Eating the alphabet: Fruits and vegetables from A to Z* (1st ed.). San Diego, CA: Harcourt.

Ehlert, L. (1990). *Color farm.* New York, NY: Lippincott.

Ehlert, L. (1996a). *Feathers for lunch / Plumas para almorzar.* New York, NY: Libros Viajeros.

Ehlert, L. (1996b). *Growing vegetable soup / A sembrar sopa de verduras).* San Diego, CA: Libros Viajeros.

Ehlert, L. (1998). *Top cat.* Orlando, FL: Harcourt Children's Books.

Ehlert, L. (2001). *Waiting for wings.* San Diego, CA: Harcourt.

Ehlert, L. (2004a). *Growing vegetable soup* (1st R Wagon Books ed.). San Diego, CA: Harcourt.

Ehlert, L. (2004b). *Pie in the sky* (1st ed.). Orlando, FL: Harcourt.

Ehlert, L. (2006). *In my world.* New York, NY: Harcourt.

Emberley, E. (1972). *Drawing book: Make a world* (1st ed.). Boston, MA: Little, Brown.

Emberley, E. (2005a). *Ed Emberley's drawing book of trucks and trains.* New York, NY: LB Kids.

Emberley, E. (2005b). *Ed Emberley's picture pie two.* New York, NY: LB Kids.

Emberley, E. (2006a). *Ed Emberley's big green drawing book.* New York, NY: LB Kids.

Emberley, E. (2006b). *Ed Emberley's big purple drawing book.* New York, NY: LB Kids.

Emberley, E. (2006c). *Ed Emberley's drawing book: Make a world* (1st rev. paperback ed.). New York, NY: Little, Brown.

Emberley, E. (2006d). *Ed Emberley's drawing book of animals.* New York, NY: LB Kids.

Emberley, E. (2006e). *Ed Emberley's drawing book of faces.* New York, NY: LB Kids.

Emberley, E. (2006f). *Ed Emberley's picture pie* (reissue). New York, NY: LB Kids.

Emberley, R. (2004). *Piñata* (bilingual ed.). New York, NY Little, Brown Young Readers.

Emberley, R. (2005). *My food / Mi comida.* New York, NY: LB kids.

Emberley, R. (2008). *My garden / Mi jardín.* New York, NY: LB kids.

Ernst, L. C. (2008). *Round like a ball!* Maplewood, NJ: Blue Apple Books.

Evans, S. (2011). *Underground: Finding the light to freedom.* Brookfield, CT: Roaring Brook Press.

Facklam, M. (2002). *Bugs for lunch/Insectos para el almuerzo* Watertown, MA: Charlesbridge.

Falwell, C. (2008). *Feast for 10.* New York, NY: Clarion Books. .

Falwell, C. (2009). *Mystery vine: A pumpkin surprise.* New York, NY: HarperCollins.

Farjeon, E. (2010). *Cats sleep anywhere.* London, UK: Frances Lincoln Children's Books.

Farjeon, E., & Ladwig, T. (1996). *Morning has broken.* Grand Rapids, MI: Eerdmans.

Feliciano, J. (2003). *Feliz navidad.* Sedona, AZ: J & H.

Felix, M. (1994). *Plane (mouse books).* Orlando, FL: Harcourt Brace.

Felix, M. (2012). *The wind.* Mankato, MN: Creative Editions.

Fisher, D. (2007). *Insects: Step-by-step instructions for 26 creepy crawlies.* Irvine, CA: Walter Foster.

Flatharta, A. (2009). *Hurry and the monarch* (reprint ed.) New York, NY: Dragonfly Books.

Fleming, D. (1991). *In the tall, tall grass* (1st ed.). New York, NY: Henry Holt.

Fleming, D. (1992). *Lunch* (1st ed.). New York, NY: Henry Holt.

Fleming, D. (1998). *Mama cat has three kittens* (1st ed.). New York, NY: Henry Holt.

Fleming, D. (2001). *Time to sleep.* New York, NY: Henry Holt.

Fleming, D. (2007). *Beetle bop.* Orlando, FL: Harcourt.

Fleming, D. (2008). *Buster.* New York, NY: Henry Holt.

Fleming, D. (2011). *Shout! Shout it out!* New York, NY: Henry Holt.

Ford, M., & Noll, S. (1995). *Sunflower.* New York, NY: Greenwillow Books.

Foreman, J., & Foreman, M. (2008). *Say hello.* Cambridge, MA: Candlewick Press.

Fox, M. (1983). *Hattie and the fox.* New York, NY: Bradbury Press.

Fox, M. (2002). *Quienquiera que seas.* New York, NY: Harcourt.

Fox, M. (2006). *Whoever you are* (Reading Rainbow Books). New York, NY: Voyager Harcourt.

French, J. (2003). *Diary of a wombat.* New York, NY: Clarion Books.

French, J. (2007). *Too many pears* (bilingual English/Japanese ed.). Long Island City, NY: Star Bright Books.

French, V. (2010). *Yucky worms.* Somerville, MA: Candlewick Press.

Frost, H. (2008). *Monarch and milkweed.* New York, NY: Atheneum Books for Young Readers.

Fucile, T. (2009). *Let's do nothing.* Somerville, MA: Candlewick Press.

Galdone, P. (2011). *The three little kittens* (Folk Tale Classics). New York, NY: Houghton Mifflin Harcourt.

Ganeri, A. (2007). *Butterflies and caterpillars* (Animals and Their Babies series). Mankato, MN: Smart Apple Media.

Gershator, D., Gershator, P., & Shaw-Smith, E. (1998). *Bread is for eating* (1st ed.). New York, NY: Henry Holt.

Gerth, M. (2005a). *Five little ladybugs.* Los Angeles, CA: Piggy Toes.

Gerth, M. (2005b). *Ten little ladybugs.* Los Angeles, CA: Piggy Toes.

Gibbons, G. (1987). *Las vacas lecheras / The milk makers* New York, NY: Aladdin.

Gibbons, G. (1991). *Monarch butterfly.* New York, NY: Holiday House.

Giganti, P., & Crews, D. (1992). *Each orange had 8 slices: A counting book* (1st ed.). New York, NY: Greenwillow Books.

Giganti, P., & Crews, D. (2005). *How many blue birds flew away?: A counting book with a difference* (1st ed.). New York, NY: Greenwillow Books.

Gilchrist, J. S. (2007). *My America.* New York, NY: Harper Collins.

Ginsburg, M. (2000). *The chick and the duckling* (Translated from the Russian of V. Suteyev). New York, NY: Scholastic.

Giovanni, N. (1994). *Knoxville, Tennessee.* New York, NY: Scholastic.

Glaser, L. (1994). *Wonderful worms.* Brookfield, CT: Millbrook.

Glaser, L. (2003). *Brilliant bees.* Brookfield, CT: Millbrook.

Glaser, L. (2008). *Dazzling dragonflies: A life cycle Story.* Brookfield, CT: Millbrook.

Goodall, J. (1999). *The surprise picnic.* New York, NY: Margaret K. McElderry.

Graham, C. (1978). *Jazz chants.* New York, NY: Oxford University Press.

Greenfield, E. (2002). *Honey, I love.* New York, NY: HarperCollins.

Guettier, B. (2005). *Dinosaurs/Dinosaures.* (1st American ed.). San Diego, CA: Kane/Miller.

Guthrie, W., & Jakobsen, K. (2002). *This land is your land* (1st ed.). Boston, MA: Little, Brown.

Hall, M. (2010). *My heart is like a zoo.* New York, NY: Greenwillow Books.

Hall, Z., & Halpern, S. (1994). *It's pumpkin time!* New York, NY: Blue Sky Press.

Hall, Z., & Halpern, S. (1996). *The apple pie tree.* New York, NY: Scholastic.

Hall, Z., & Halpern, S. (2002). *It's pumpkin time!/Tiempo de calabazas.* New York, NY: Blue Sky Press.

Harper, C. M. (2005). *The little book of not so: A book of opposites.* New York, NY: Houghton Mifflin.

Harter, D., & Blackstone, S. (2004). *Walking through the jungle.* Cambridge, MA: Barefoot Books.

Havill, J. (2009). *Just like a baby.* San Francisco, CA: Chronicle Books.

Heiligman, D., & Weissman, B. (1995). *From caterpillar to butterfly.* New York, NY: HarperCollins.

Heller, R. (1992). *How to hide a butterfly and other insects.* New York, NY: Grosset & Dunlap.

Henkes, K. (2004). *Kitten's first full moon* (7th ed.). New York, NY: Greenwillow Books.

Hickman, P., & Collins, H. (1997a). *A new butterfly: My first look at metamorphosis* (My First Look at Nature series). Tonawanda, NY: Kids Can Press.

Hickman, P., & Collins, H. (1997b). *A seed grows: My first look at a plant's life cycle* (My First Look at Nature series). Tonawanda, NY: Kids Can Press.

Highwater, J. (1995). *Songs for the seasons* (1st ed.). New York, NY: HarperCollins.

Hill, M. (2002). *Let's make pizza* (Welcome Books in the Kitchen). New York, NY: Children's Press.

Himmelman, J. (1998). *A luna moth's life* (Nature Upclose series). New York, NY: Children's Press.

Himmelman, J. (1999). *A dandelion's life* (Nature Upclose series). New York, NY: Children's Press.

Himmelman, J. (2000). *A monarch butterfly's life* (Nature Upclose series). New York, NY: Children's Press.

Holmes, J. (2009). *There was an old lady who swallowed a fly.* San Francisco, CA: Chronicle Books.

Holmes, M. T., & Harris, J. (2010). *A giraffe goes to Paris.* Tarrytown, NY: Marshall Cavendish Children.

Holub, J. (2001). *The pizza that we made.* New York, NY: Viking Puffin Books.

Hood, S. (2003). *Caterpillar spring, butterfly summer.* New York, NY: Readers Digest.

Hoose, P., & Hoose, H. (1998). *Hey, little ant.* Berkeley, CA: Tricycle Press.

Horacek, P. (2001). *Strawberries are red (look inside)* (board book ed.). New York, NY: Walker Children's Hardbacks.

Hubbell, P. (2004). *I like cats.* New York, NY: North South.

Hubbell, P., Halsey, M., & Addy, S. (2006). *Cars: Rushing! honking! zooming!* New York, NY: Marshall Cavendish.

Hubbell, P., Halsey, M., & Addy, S. (2008). *Airplanes: Soaring! diving! turning!* (1st ed.). New York, NY: Marshall Cavendish.

Huggins-Cooper, L. (2005). *Alien invaders/Invasores extraterrestres.* Green Bay, WI: Raven Tree Press.

Huggins-Cooper, L. (2010). *Alien invaders* (1st ed. .). Green Bay, WI: Raven Tree Press.

Hughes, L. (2009a). *My people.* New York, NY: Atheneum Books for Young Readers.

Hughes, L. (2009b). *The Negro speaks of rivers.* New York, NY: Disney Jump at the Sun.

Hutchins, P. (1982). *1 hunter* (1st ed.). New York, NY: Greenwillow Books.

Hutchins, P. (1986). *The doorbell rang* (1st ed.). New York, NY: Greenwillow Books.

Hutchins, P. (1987). *Changes, changes* (1st Aladdin Books ed.). New York, NY: Aladdin Books.

Hutchins, P. (2000). *Ten red apples.* New York, NY: Greenwillow Books.

Hutchins, P. (2002). *We're going on a picnic.* New York, NY: Greenwillow Books.

Numeroff, L. (1995). *If you give a mouse a cookie.* New York, NY: HarperCollins.

Numeroff, L. (2010). *If you give a cat a cupcake.* New York, NY: HarperCollins.

IKids. (2009). *Green start: In the garden* (Board Book ed.). Norwalk, CT: Innovative Kids.

Isadora, R. (2009). *Happy belly, happy smile.* New York, NY: Houghton Mifflin Harcourt.

Iwamura, K., & Carle, E. (2003). *Where are you going? To see my friend! A story of friendship in two languages* (English and Japanese). New York, NY: Scholastic.

James, S. (1996). *Dear Mr. Blueberry.* New York, NY: Margaret K. McElderry.

Jenkins, E., & Bogacki, T. (2005). *Five creatures.* New York, NY: Farrar, Straus and Giroux.

Jenkins, S. (2004). *Actual size.* Boston, MA: Houghton Mifflin.

Jenkins, S., & Page, R. (2003). *What do you do with a tail like this?* Boston, MA: Houghton Mifflin.

Jones, B. (1998). *Dance.* New York, NY: Hyperion Books for Children.

Kalan, R. (2002). *Jump, frog, jump!* New York, NY: HarperFestival.

Kavanaugh, M., & Gurman, S. (2009). *Snapshot picture library: Kittens.* San Francisco, CA: Fog City Books.

Keats, E. J. (1999). *Clementina's cactus.* New York, NY: Viking, Penguin Putnam Books for Young Readers.

Kelly, M. (2000). *The ants came marching* (board book ed.). Brooklyn, NY: Handprint Books.

Kerley, B. (2002). *A cool drink of water.* Washington, DC: National Geographic Society.

Kerley, B. (2005). *You and me together: Moms, dads, and kids around the world.* Washington, D.C.: National Geographic.

Kerley, B. (2007). *Peace.* Washington, DC: National Geographic.

Kim, S. (2010). *How does a seed grow? A book with foldout pages.* New York, NY: Little Simon.

Kitamura, S. (1996). *Cat is sleepy* (board book ed.) New York, NY: Farrar, Straus and Giroux.

Kraus, R. (1988). *The carrot seed.* New York, NY: Harper Collins.

Kraus, R. (1996). *La semilla de zanahoria/The carrot seed.* New York, NY: Harper Collins.

Legg, G. (1998). *From caterpillar to butterfly* (Lifecycles series). Danbury, CT: Children's Press.

Legg, G., & Scrace, C. (1998). *From seed to sunflower* (Lifecycles series). (1st American ed.). New York, NY: Franklin Watts.

Lehman, B. (2004). *The red book.* Boston, MA: Houghton Mifflin.

Leslie, A. (2000). *Do crocodiles moo?* (A Lift-the-Flap Book). San Francisco, CA: Chronicle Books.

Lewison, W. (2000). *One little butterfly.* New York, NY: Grosset & Dunlap.

Lin, G. (2002). *Kite flying.* New York, NY: Alfred A. Knopf.

Lin, G. (2003). *Dim sum for everyone.* New York, NY: Alfred A. Knopf.

Ling, M. (2007). *Butterfly. See how they grow.* New York, NY: DK Publishing.

Litwin, E. (2010). *Pete the cat: I love my white shoes.* New York, NY: HarperCollins.

Litwin, E. (2011). *Pete the cat: Rocking in my school shoes.* New York, NY: HarperCollins.

Ljungkvist, L. (2006). *Follow the line.* New York, NY: Viking.

Ljungkvist, L. (2007). *Follow the line through the house.* New York, NY: Viking.

Ljungkvist, L. (2008). *Follow the line around the world.* New York, NY: Viking.

Ljungkvist, L. (2011). *Follow the line to school.* New York, NY: Viking.

Lobel, A. (1989). *On market street* (25th anniversary ed.). New York, NY: Greenwillow Books.

Locker, T. (2001). *Mountain dance* (1st ed.). San Diego, CA: Harcourt.

Locker, T. (2002). *Water dance* (1st ed.). San Diego, CA: Harcourt.

Lujan, J., & Monroy, M. (2004). *Rooster/Gallo.* Berkeley, CA: Groundwood Books.

Luxbacher, I. (2008). *123 I can make prints* (Starting Art series). Toronto, ON: Kids Can Press.

Maass, R. (2011). *A is for autumn.* New York, NY: Henry Holt.

Maccarone, G. (1994). *Pizza party* (Hello Reader). New York, NY: Cartwheel.

Marley, C. (2011). *One love.* San Francisco, CA: Chronicle Books.

Martin, B. Jr., & Carle, E. (1992). *Brown bear, brown bear, what do you see?* New York, NY: Henry Holt.

Marzollo, J. (1996). *I'm a seed* (Hello Reader). New York, NY: Cartwheel.

Marzollo, J. (1997). *I'm a caterpillar.* New York, NY: Cartwheel.

Marzollo, J., & Wick, W. (2006). *I spy a butterfly.* New York, NY: Scholastic.

Masiello, R. (2004). *Ralph Masiello's Bug drawing book.* Watertown, MA: Charlesbridge.

Masurel, C., & Kolar, B. (2001). *A cat and a dog.* New York, NY: North South Books.

McCarty, P. (2008). *Hondo and Fabian.* New York, NY: Square Fish.

McDonnell, P. (2005). *The gift of nothing* (1st ed.). New York, NY: Little, Brown.

McPhail, D. (1998). *A bug, a bear, and a boy.* New York, NY: Scholastic.

Micklethwait, L. (1998). *I spy two eyes: Numbers in art.* New York, NY: Greenwillow Books.

Micklethwait, L. (2004). *I spy shapes in art.* New York, NY: Greenwillow Books.

Miller, D. (2001). *Just like you and me.* New York, NY: Dial Books for Young Readers.

Miller, M. (1990). *Who uses this?.* New York, NY: Greenwillow Books.

Monks, L. (2007). *Aaaarrgghh! spider!.* New York, NY: Houghton Mifflin.

Moore, I. (1991). *Six-dinner Sid.* New York, NY: Simon & Schuster.

Moore, I. (2011). *Six-dinner Sid: A highland adventure.* New York, NY: Aladdin.

Moore, M. (2006). *The wheels on the school bus* (1st ed.). New York, NY: HarperCollins.

Mora, P. (1994). *The desert is my mother / El desierto es mi madre.* Houston, TX: Piñata Books.

Morris, A. (1993a). *Bread, bread, bread.* New York, NY: Harper-Collins.

Morris, A. (1993b). *Hats, hats, hats* (1st Mulberry ed.). New York, NY: Mulberry Books.

Munsch, R. (1988). *Angela's airplane* (Annikin ed.) Toronto, ON: Annick Press.

Myers, C. (1999). *Black cat.* New York, NY: Scholastic.

Myers, S., & Walker, D. (2007). *Kittens! Kittens! Kittens!* New York, NY: Harry N. Abrams.

Neitzel, S. (1994). *The jacket I wear in the snow* (1st ed.). New York, NY: Greenwillow Books.

Neitzel, S. (1995). *The dress I'll wear to the party* (1st ed.). New York, NY: Greenwillow Books.

Neitzel, S. (1997). *The house I'll build for the wrens* (1st ed.). New York, NY: Greenwillow Books.

Neitzel, S., & Parker, N. W. (1997). *We're making breakfast for Mother* (1st ed.). New York, NY: Greenwillow Books.

Neitzel, S., & Parker, N. W. (1998). *The bag I'm taking to Grandma's* (1st ed.). New York, NY: Greenwillow Books.

Neubecker, R. (2006). *Wow! America!* (1st ed.). New York, NY: Hyperion Books for Children.

Newgarden, M. (2007). *Bow-Wow bugs a bug.* New York, NY: Harcourt.

Niepold, M., & Verdu, J. (2007). *Oooh! Matisse.* Berkeley, CA: Tricycle Press.

Niepold, M., & Verdu, J. (2009). *Oooh! Picasso.* Berkeley, CA: Tricycle Press.

Nolan, H. (1995). *How much, how many, how far, how heavy, how long, how tall is 1000?* Toronto, ON, Canada: Kids Can Press.

Novick, M., & Hale, J. (2002). *Double delight animals.* New York, NY: Backpack Books.

Novick, M., & Hale, J. (2003). *Double delight bugs.* New York, NY: Backpack Books.

Numeroff, L. (2010). *If you give a cat a cupcake/Si le das un pastelito a un gato.* New York, NY: Rayo/Laura Geringer Books.

Núñez, A. (2004). *Dime traviesa ¿que frusta es esa?/Tell me mischievous, what fruit is that?* Mexico D.F., Mexico: Centro de Informacion y Desarollo de la Comunicacion y la Literatura Infantil (CIDCLE).

Oliver, N. (2009). *Twilight hunt: A seek-and-find book.* Long Island City, NY: Star Bright Books.

Orloff, K. K. (2004). *I wanna iguana.* New York, NY: Putnam.

Page, G. (2011). *How to be a good cat.* New York, NY: Bloomsbury USA Children's.

Page, R., & Jenkins, S. (2006). *Move!* Boston, MA: Houghton Mifflin.

Paley, J. (2002). *One more river: A Noah's Ark counting book.* New York, NY: Megan Tingley.

Parr, T. (2010). *The earth book.* New York, NY: Little, Brown Books for Young Readers.

Pattison, D. (2003). *The journey of Oliver K. Woodman.* San Diego, CA: Harcourt.

Pattou, E. (2001). *Mrs. Spitzer's garden.* Orlando, FL: Harcourt.

Peck, J. (2005). *Way up high in a tall green tree* (1st ed.). New York, NY: Simon & Schuster Books for Young Readers.

Perdomo, W. (2002). *Visiting Langston.* New York, NY: Henry Holt.

Pinkney, J. (2009). *The lion and the mouse* (1st ed.). New York, NY: Little, Brown Books for Young Readers.

Pinto, S. (2008). *Apples and oranges: Going bananas with pairs.* New York, NY: Bloomsbury USA Children's.

Play Bac. (2007). *EyeLike: Numbers.* New York, NY: Play Bac.

Play Bac. (2008). *Baby EyeLike: Triangle.* New York, NY: Play Bac.

Pollock, P. (2001). *When the moon is full: A lunar year.* New York, NY: Little Brown.

Pomeroy, D. (2000). *One potato: A counting book of potato prints.* New York, NY: Voyager.

Portis, A. (2006). *Not a box.* New York, NY: HarperCollins.

Posada, M. (2007). *Ladybugs: Red, fiery, and bright.* New York, NY: First Avenue Editions.

Prelutsky, J., & Rand, T. (2004). *If not for the cat: Haiku* (1st ed.). New York, NY: Greenwillow Books.

Priceman, M. (1994). *How to make an apple pie and see the world.* New York, NY: Alfred A. Knopf.

Prince, A. (2006). *What do wheels do all day?* Boston, MA: Houghton Mifflin Books for Children.

Raczka, B. (2002). *No one saw: Ordinary things through the eyes of an artist.* Brookfield, CT: Millbrook Press.

Raczka, B. (2010). *Guyku: A year of haiku for boys.* Boston, MA: Houghton Mifflin.

Raffi. (1990). *The wheels on the bus* (Raffi Songs to Read series) (1st ed.). New York, NY: Crown Books for Young Readers.

Raffi. (1996). *Spider on the floor* (Raffi Songs to Read series). New York, NY: Crown Books for Young Readers.

Ravishankar, A. (2004). *Tiger on a tree.* New York, NY: Farrar, Straus and Giroux.

Reiser, L. (1998). *Tortillas and lullabies / Tortillas y cancioncitas* (1st ed.). New York, NY: Greenwillow Books.

Reiser, L. (2001). *My cat tuna.* New York, NY: Greenwillow Books.

Ringgold, F. (2004). *Cassie's word quilt.* New York, NY: Alfred A. Knopf.

Rockwell, A. (1996). *Sweet potato pie.* New York, NY: Random House.

Rockwell, A. (1999). *One bean.* New York, NY: Walker Children's.

Rockwell, A. (2001). *Bugs are insects.* New York, NY: Harper Collins.

Root, P. (2000). *Hey, tabby cat!* (Brand New Readers series). Cambridge, MA: Candlewick Press.

Rosa-Mendoza, G. (2002). *Fruits and vegetables/Frutas y vegetales.* Wheaton, IL: Me+Mi.

Ross, K. (2009). *Crafts for kids who are learning about insects.* Minneapolis, MN: Millbrook Press.

Ross, K. (2006). *Crafts for kids who are learning about transportation.* Minneapolis, MN: Millbrook Press.

Rotner, S., & Hellum, J. (1996). *Hold the anchovies! A book about pizza.* New York, NY: Orchard Books.

Rubin, S. G. (2008). *Matisse dance for joy.* San Francisco, CA: Chronicle Books.

Rumford, J. (2001). *Traveling man: The journey of Ibn Battuta, 1325–1354.* Boston, MA: Houghton Mifflin.

Rylant, C. (2005). *If you'll be my valentine.* New York, NY: HarperCollins.

Segal, J. (2006). *Carrot soup.* New York, NY: Margaret K. McElderry Books.

Serafini, F. (2008). *Looking closely through the forest.* Tonawanda, NY: Kids Can Press.

Serfozo, M., & Narahashi, K. (1996). *What's what? A guessing game* (1st ed.). New York, NY: Margaret K. McElderry Books.

Seuss, Dr. (2004). *Ten apples up on top!* New York, NY: Beginner Books.

Seuss, Dr., & Johnson, S. (1998). *My many colored days.* New York, NY: Alfred A. Knopf.

Seuss, Dr., & Mathieu, J. (1999). *The eye book* (Bright and Early Books). New York, NY: Random House.

Shange, N. (2009). *Coretta Scott.* New York, NY: Katherine Tegen Books.

Shannon, G. (1999). *Tomorrow's alphabet.* New York, NY: Greenwillow Books.

Shulevitz, U. (1988). *Dawn.* New York, NY: Farrar, Straus and Giroux.

Sis, P. (1999). *Ships ahoy.* New York, NY: Farrar, Straus and Giroux.

Slate, J. (2009). *I want to be free.* New York, NY: G. P. Putnam's Sons.

Smith, M. (2002). *Dear Daisy, get well soon.* New York, NY: Dragonfly Books.

Soltis, S. (2011). *Nothing like a puffin.* Cambridge, MA: Candlewick Press.

Spier, P. (1982). *Peter Spier's rain* (1st ed.). Garden City, NY: Doubleday.

Spier, P. (1987). *Noah's ark.* Garden City, NY: Doubleday.

Stewart, A. E. (1999). *Who's hiding in the garden?* (Wobbly-Eyed Lift-the-Flap book) New York, NY: Parragon Book Service.

Sturges, P. (2005). *I love bugs!* New York, NY: HarperCollins.

Sturges, P., & Halpern, S. (2003). *I love planes!* (1st ed.). New York, NY: Harper Collins.

Swain, G. (1999a). *Carrying* (Small World series). Minneapolis, MN: Carolrhoda.

Swain, G. (1999b). *Celebrating* (Small World series). Minneapolis, MN: Carolrhoda.

Swain, G. (1999c). *Eating* (Small World series). Minneapolis, MN: Carolrhoda.

Swain, G. (1999d). *Smiling.* (Small World series). Minneapolis, MN: Carolrhoda.

Sweeney, J. (1996). *Me on the map* (1st ed.). New York, NY: Crown.

Sweeney, J. (2000). *Me and my family tree.* New York, NY: Crown.

Taback, S. (1997). *There was an old lady* (Caldecott Honor Book) New York, NY: Viking.

Taback, S. (1999). *Joseph had a little overcoat.* New York, NY: Viking.

Tan, S. (2007). *The arrival.* New York, NY: Arthur A. Levine Books.

Thompson, L. (2007). *The apple pie that Papa baked.* New York, NY: Simon & Schuster Books for Young Readers.

Thomson, S. (2005). *Imagine a day.* New York, NY: Atheneum.

Titherington, J. (1986). *Pumpkin, pumpkin.* New York, NY: Greenwillow Books.

Tokuda, Y. (2006). *I'm a pill bug.* San Diego, CA: Kane/Miller.

Trasler, J. (2011). *Caveman: A B.C. story.* New York, NY: Sterling.

Tullet, H. (2005). *Night/day: A book of eye-catching opposites.* London, UK: Milet.

Turhan, S. (2003). *Milet mini picture dictionary* (Available in bilingual editions with English paired with Chinese, Farsi, Korean, Kurdish, Russian, Somali, Turkish, and Urdu). Chicago, IL: Milet.

Turhan, S. (2005). *Milet picture dictionary* (Available in bilingual editions with English paired with Chinese, Farsi, Korean, Kurdish, Russian, Somali, Turkish, and Urdu). Chicago, IL: Milet.

Tusa, R. (2011). *Follow me.* Boston, MA: Harcourt Children's Books.

Vaccaro Seeger, L. (2004). *Lemons are not red.* New York, NY: Roaring Brook Press.

Van Laan, N. (2002). *A tree for me.* New York, NY: Dragonfly Books.

Vega, D. (2008). *Build a burrito: A counting book in English and Spanish.* New York, NY: Cartwheel.

Volkmann, R. (2001). *Curious kittens.* New York, NY: Random House Children's Books.

Waite, J. (1999). *Mouse, look out!* La Jolla, CA: Little Tiger Press.

Wallace, K. (1999). *Busy Buzzy Bee* (DK Readers series). New York, NY: DK.

Wallace, K. (2000). *Born to Be a butterfly* (DK Readers series). New York, NY: DK.

Walsh, E. S. (1996). *Hop, jump/Salta y brinca.* Madison, WI: Demco Media.

Walsh, M. (1996). *Do pigs have stripes?* Lawrence, KS: Mammoth/Egmont.

Wang, M., Schneider, C. M., & Runnells, T. (2005). *Who stole the cookie from the cookie jar?* Los Angeles, CA: Piggy Toes Press.

Watt, F. (2000). *That's not my plane* (Touchy-Feely Board Book series). London, UK: Usborne.

Watt, F. (2001a). *Este no es mi gatito/ That's not my kitten: Tiene las orejas blandas (Toca toca!).* London, UK: Usborne.

Watt, F. (2001b). *That's not my kitten: Its ears are too soft.* (Touchy-Feely Board Book series). London, UK: Usborne.

Weiss, G., Thiele, B., & Bryan, A. (1995). *What a wonderful world* (1st ed.). New York, NY: Atheneum Books for Young Readers.

Weiss, N. (2000). *The world turns round and round* (1st ed.). New York, NY: Greenwillow Books.

Wellington, M. (2001). *Apple farmer Annie.* New York, NY: Dutton.

Wellington, M. (2006). *Pizza at Sally's* New York, NY: Dutton.

Westcott, N. B. (1992). *Peanut butter and jelly: A play rhyme.* New York, NY: Puffin.

Willems, M. (2004). *The pigeon finds a hot dog!* (1st ed.). New York, NY: Hyperion Books for Children.

Willems, M. (2010). *Cat the cat, who is that?* (1st ed.). New York, NY: Balzer Bray.

Wing, N. (2000). *The night before Valentine's Day* New York, NY: Grosset & Dunlap.

Wood, A. (1997). *Quick as a cricket.* New York, NY: Child's Play.

Yolen, J., & Schoenherr, J. (1987). *Owl moon.* New York, NY: Philomel Books.

Ziefert, H. (2002). *Kitty says meow!* New York, NY: Grosset & Dunlap.

Ziefert, H. (2003). *31 uses for a mom.* New York, NY: G. P. Putnam's Sons.

Ziefert, H., & Brand, O. (2007). *When I first came to this land.* New York, NY: Putnam Juvenile.

Professional References and Resources

Allen, V. (1994). Selecting materials for the reading instruction of ESL children. In K. Spangenberg-Urbschat & R. Pritchard (Eds.), *Kids come in all languages: Reading instruction for ESL students* (pp. 108–134). Newark, DE: International Reading Association.

Allen, R. V. (1976). *Language experiences in communication.* Boston, MA: Houghton Mifflin.

Allen, R. V., & Allen, C. (1976). *Language experience activities.* Boston, MA: Houghton Mifflin.

Anstey, M. (2002). *More than cracking the code: Postmodern picture books and new literacies.* In M. Anstey & G. Bull (Eds.), *Crossing the boundaries* (pp. 87–105). Melbourne, Victoria, Australia: Deakin University Press.

Asher, J. J. (1986). *Learning another language through actions: The complete teacher's guidebook* (3rd ed.). Los Gatos, CA: Sky Oaks.

Auerbach, E. (1999). The power of writing, the writing of power. *Focus on Basics, 3*(D). Retrieved from http://www.ncsall.net/index.php?id=341

August, D., & Shanahan, T. (2006). *Developing literacy in second language learners: Report of the national literacy panel on language-minority children and youth.* New York: Routledge.

Benedict, S., & Carlisle, L. (1992). *Beyond words: Picture books for older readers and writers.* Portsmouth, NH: Heinemann.

Boyd–Batstone, P. (2006). *Differentiated early literacy for English language learners: Practical strategies.* Boston, MA: Allyn & Bacon.

Bownan-Perrott, L. J., Herrera, S., & Murry, K. (2010). Reading difficulties and grade retention: What's the connection for English language learners? *Reading & Writing Quarterly, 26*(1), 91–107.

Calderon, M. (2005, November-December). *Evidence-based program for ELLs* [PowerPoint presentation]. Fourth Annual Celebrate Our Rising Stars Summit, Office of English Language Acquisition, U.S. Department of Education, Washington, D.C.

Calderon, M. (2007). *Teaching reading to English language learners, grades 6–12: A framework for improving achievement in the content areas.* Thousand Oaks, CA: Corwin.

Calkins, L. (1994). *The art of teaching writing.* Portsmouth, NH: Heinemann.

Canale, M. (1983). Readability in ESL. *Reading in a Foreign Language, 4*(1), 21–40.

Chafe, W., & Danielewicz, J. (1987). Properties of spoken and written language. In R. Horowitz & S. J. Samuels (Eds.), *Comprehending oral and written language* (pp. 83–113). San Diego, CA: Academic Press.

Chamot, A. (2005). The cognitive academic language learning approach (CALLA): An update. In R. Amato & M. Snow (Eds.), *Academic success for English language learners* (pp. 87–102). New York, NY: Longman.

Chamot, A., & O'Malley, M. (1994). Instructional approaches and teaching procedures. In K. Spangenberg-Urbschat & R. Pritchard (Eds.), *Kids come in all languages: Reading instruction for ESL students* (pp. 82–106). Newark, DE: International Reading Association.

Chaudron, C. (1988). *Second language classrooms: Research on teaching and learning.* Cambridge, UK: Cambridge University Press.

Cienchanowski, K. (2009). "A squirrel came and pushed earth": Popular culture and scientific ways of thinking for ELLs. *The Reading Teacher, 62*(7), 558–568.

Coggins, D., Kravin, D., Coats, G. D., & Carroll, M. D. (2007). *English language learners in the mathematics classroom.* Thousand Oaks, CA: Corwin.

Cox, C. (2005). *Teaching language arts: A student- and response-centered classroom* (5th ed.). Boston, MA: Allyn & Bacon.

Cox, C., & Boyd-Batstone, P. (2009). *Engaging English learners: Exploring literature, developing literacy, and differentiating instruction.* Saddle River, NJ: Prentice–Hall.

Cummins, J. (1981). The role of primary language development in promoting educational success for language minority students. In California State Department of Education, *Schooling and language minority students* (pp. 3–49). Los Angeles: California State University, Center for Research, Evaluation, Assessment, and Dissemination.

Cummins, J. (1991). Interdependence of first- and second-language proficiency in bilingual children. In E. Bialystok (Ed.), *Language processing in bilingual children* (pp. 70–89). Cambridge, UK: Cambridge University Press.

Curtain, H., & Dahlberg, C. (2010). *Languages and children: Making the match: New languages for young learners, grades K–8* (4th ed.). Boston, MA: Allyn & Bacon.

de Oliveira, L. (2010). Enhancing content instruction for English language learners: Learning about language in science. In D. Sunal, C. Sunal, & E. Wright (Eds.), *Teaching science with Hispanic ELLs in K–16 classrooms* (pp. 135–149). Charlotte, NC: Information Age.

de Oliveira, L. Hadaway, N. L., & Mundy, J. (2010). Enhancing content instruction for English language learners: Learning about language in science. In D. Sunal, C. Sunal, & E. Wright (Eds.), *Teaching science with Hispanic ELLs in K–16 classrooms* (pp. 135–149). Charlotte, NC: IAP-Information Age.

Deeb, I., & Jakar, V. (2009). The book after a book project: Aspects of teaching English as a foreign language. In D. Meier (Ed.), *Here's the story: Using narrative to promote young children's language and literacy learning* (pp. 92–106). New York, NY: Teachers College Press.

Delpit, L. D. (2006). *Other people's children: Cultural conflict in the classroom* (2nd ed.). New York, NY: The New Press.

Dutro, S., & Moran, C. (2005). Rethinking English language instruction: An architectural approach. In G. G. Garcia (Ed.), *English learners: Reading the highest level of English literacy* (pp. 227–258). Upper Saddle River, NJ: Merrill Education and International Reading Association.

Early, M. (1991). Using wordless picture books to promote second language learning. *English Language Teaching Journal, 45*(3), 245–251.

Echevarria, J. (2011). *Sheltered content instruction: Teaching English language learners with diverse abilities* (4th ed.). Boston, MA: Pearson.

Echevarria, J., & Graves, A. (2007). *Sheltered content instruction: Teaching English language learners with diverse abilities* (3rd ed.). Toronto, ON: Pearson Education.

Echevarria, J., Vogt, M. E., & Short, D. (2008). *Making content comprehensible for English learners: The SIOP® Model.* Boston, MA: Allyn & Bacon.

Ellis, R. (2008). *Principles of instructed second language acquisition.* Center for Applied Linguistics online resources. Retrieved from http://www.cal.org/resources/digest/instructed2ndlang.html

Fountas, I. C., & Pinnell, G. S. (2005). *Leveled books, K–8: Matching texts to readers for effective teaching.* Portsmouth, NH: Heinemann.

Fountas, I. C., Pinnell, G. S., & Bird, L. B. (1999). *Matching books to readers: Using leveled books in guided reading, K–3.* Portsmouth, NH: Heinemann.

Fowler, G. (1982). Developing comprehension skills in primary students through the use of story frames. *The Reading Teacher, 36*(2), 176–179.

Fries, C. (1945). *Teaching & learning English as a foreign language.* Ann Arbor: University of Michigan Press.

Fry, E. (2002). Readability versus leveling. *The Reading Teacher, 56*(3), 286–297.

Galda, L., Culllihan, B., & Sipe, L. (2010). *Literature and the child.* Belmont, CA: Wadsworth.

García, G. G., & Beltran, D. (2003). Revisioning the blueprint: Building for the academic success of English learners. In G. G. García (Ed.) *English learners: Reaching the highest level of English literacy* (pp. 197–226). Newark, DE: International Reading Association.

Genesee, F., Lindholm–Leary, K., Saunders, W., & Christian, D. (2005). English language learners in U.S. schools: An overview of research findings. *Journal of Education for Students Placed at Risk, 10*(4), 363–385.

Gibbons, P. (2002). *Scaffolding language, scaffolding learning: Teaching second language learners in the mainstream classroom.* Portsmouth, NH: Heinemann.

Glandon, S. (2000a). *Caldecott connections to language arts.* Englewood, CO: Libraries Unlimited.

Glandon, S. (2000b). *Caldecott connections to science.* Westport, CT: Libraries Unlimited.

Glandon, S. (2000c). *Caldecott connections to social studies.* Englewood, CO: Libraries Unlimited.

Gottlieb, M. (2006). *Assessing English language learners: Bridges from language proficiency to academic achievement.* Thousand Oaks, CA: Corwin.

Gottlieb, M., Cranely, M. E., & Oliver, A. R. (2007). *WIDA English language proficiency standards and resource guide: Prekindergarten through grade 12.* Madison, WI: University of Wisconsin–Madison, WIDA Consortium English Language.

Gouin, F. (1892/1978). *The art of teaching and studying languages* (tr. H. Swan & V. Bâetis). London, UK: G. Philip & Son.

Grabe, W., & Stroller, F. (2001). Reading for academic purposes: Guidelines for the ESL/EFL teacher. In M. Celce-Murcia (Ed.), *Teaching English as a second or foreign language* (pp. 187–203). Boston, MA: Heinle and Heinle.

Graney, J. (1992). A framework for using text graphing. *System, 20*(2), 161–167.

Gunderson, L. (2009). *ESL (ELL) literacy instruction: A guidebook to theory and practice.* New York, NY: Routledge.

Gunning, T. (1999). *Best books for teaching literacy to students.* Boston, MA: Allyn & Bacon.

Hadaway, N., & Mundy, J. (1999). Children's informational picture books visit a secondary ESL classroom. *Journal of Adolescent & Adult Literacy, 42*(6) 464–475.

Hadaway, N., Vardell, S., & Young, T. (2002). *Literature-based instruction with English language learners.* Boston, MA: Allyn & Bacon.

Hadaway, N., Vardell, S., & Young, T. (2006). Matching books and readers: Selecting literature for English learners. *Reading Teacher, 59*(8), 734–741.

Hall, S. (2001). *Using picture storybooks to teach literary devices: Recommended books for children and young adults* (vol. 3). Westport, CT: Libraries Unlimited.

Hall, S. (2007). *Using picture story books to teach literary devices: Recommended books for children and young adults* (Vol. 4). Westport, CT: Libraries Unlimited.

Hamayan, E. (1994). Language development of low literacy students. In F. Genesee (Ed.), *Educating second language children* (pp. 166–199). Cambridge, UK: Cambridge University Press.

Harris, T., & Hodges, R. (1995). *The literacy dictionary.* Newark, DE: International Reading Association.

Herman, D., Jahn, M., & Ryan, M. (Eds.). (2005). *Encyclopedia of narrative.* New York, NY, & London, UK: Routledge.

Herrell, A., & Jordan, M. (2003). *Fifty strategies for teaching English language learners* (2nd ed.). Upper Saddle River, NJ: Pearson, Merrill, Prentice-Hall.

Herrell, A., & Jordan, M. (2012). *Fifty strategies for teaching English language learners* (4th ed.). New York, NY: Allyn & Bacon.

Hickman, P. (2009). *Dynamic read-aloud strategies for English learners: Building language and literacy in the primary grades.* Newark, DE: International Reading Association.

Hickman, P., & Pollard-Durodola, S. (2009). Strategic read-aloud lessons: What the research says. In P. Hickman & S. D. Pollard-Durodola (Eds.), *Dynamic read-aloud strategies for English learners* (pp. 1–15). Newark, DE: International Reading Association.

Hickman, P., Pollard-Durodola, S., & Vaughn, S. (2004). Storybook reading: Improving vocabulary and comprehension for English-language learners. *The Reading Teacher, 57*(8), 720–730.

Hiebert, E. H., & Kamil, M. L. (2005). *Teaching and learning vocabulary: Bringing research to practice.* Mahwah, NJ: Erlbaum.

Holdaway, D. (1982). Shared book experience: Teaching reading using favorite books. *Theory Into Practice, 21*(4), 293–300.

Jacobs, G. (2003). Combining dictogloss and cooperative learning to promote language learning. *The Reading Matrix, 3*(1), 1–15. Retrieved from http://www.readingmatrix.com/articles/jacobs_small/article.pdf

Kim, H. (2006, Summer). EFL communicative language teaching within a framework of response-oriented theory. *The Journal of Asia TEFL, 3*(2), 130–140.

Kucer, S. B. (2009). *Dimensions of literacy: A conceptual base for teaching reading and writing in school settings.* New York, NY: Routledge.

Labov, W. (1972). *Language in the inner city.* University Park: University of Pennsylvania Press.

Lado, R. (1957). *Linguistics across cultures: Applied linguistics for language teachers.* Ann Arbor: University of Michigan Press.

Lado, R. (1988). *Teaching English across cultures: An introduction for teachers of English to speakers of other languages.* New York, NY: McGraw-Hill.

Laufer, B., & Paribakht, T. S. (1998). The relationship between passive and active vocabularies: Effect of language learning contexts. *Language Learning, 48*(3), 365–391.

Lemke, J. (1990). *Talking science: Language, learning, and values.* Norwood, NJ: Ablex.

Lemke, J. (1998). *Teaching all the languages of science: Words, symbols, images and actions.* Retrieved from http://academic.brooklyn.cuny.edu/education/jlemke/papers/barcelon.htm

Leuenberger, C. (2007). *Teaching early math skills with favorite picture books: Math lessons based on popular books that connect to the standards and build skills in problem solving and critical thinking.* New York, NY: Scholastic Teaching Resources.

Long, M. H. (1990a). The least a second language acquisition theory needs to explain. *TESOL Quarterly, 24*(4), 649–666.

Long, M. H. (1990b). Maturational constraints on language development. *Studies in Second Language Acquisition, 12*(3), 251–285.

Long, M. (1996). The role of linguistic environment in second language acquisition. In W. Ritchie & T. Bhatia (Eds.), *Handbook of second language acquisition* (pp. 413–468). New York, NY: Academic.

Lott, C. (2001). Picture books in the high school English classroom. In B. Ericson (Ed.), *Teaching reading in high school* (pp. 139–154). Urbana, IL: National Council of Teachers of English.

Morrow, L. (1988). Young children's responses to one-to-one story readings in school settings. *Reading Research Quarterly, 23,* 89–107.

Nasr, R. (1994). *Whole education: A new direction to fill the relevance gap.* Lanham, MD: University Press of America.

Nation, I. (2001). *Learning vocabulary in another language.* Cambridge, UK: Cambridge University Press.

Nation, I. (2008). *Teaching vocabulary: Strategies and techniques.* Boston, MA: Heinle Cengage Learning.

Nation, I., & Chung, T. (2009). Teaching and testing vocabulary. In M. H. Long & C. J. Doughty (Eds.), *The handbook of language teaching* (pp. 543–559). Hoboken, NJ: Wiley-Blackwell.

Nation, P. (1996). The four strands of a language course. *TESOL in Context, 6*(2), 7–12. Retrieved from http://www.victoria.ac.nz/lals/about/staff/publications/paul-nation/1996-Four-strands.pdf

National Reading Panel. (2000). *Report of the National Reading Panel: Teaching children to read* (NIH Publication no. 00–4754). Washington DC: U.S. Government Printing Office.

Nelson, O., & Linek, W. (1998). *Practical classroom applications of language experience: Looking back, looking forward.* Boston, MA: Allyn & Bacon.

Nessel, D. & Dixon, C. (2008). *Using the language experience approach with English language learners: Strategies for engaging students and developing literacy.* Thousand Oaks, CA: Corwin.

Nisbet, D., & Tindall, E. (2006). Ten distinctions that inform reading instruction for English language learners. *Reading in Virginia, 19,* 21–26.

Nikolajeva, M., & Scott, C. (2006). *How picturebooks work.* New York, NY: Routledge.

Nolde, R. (2008). The changing face of children's picture books: An analysis of Caldecott and children's choice award winners in the digital age. *International Journal of the Book, 6*(3), 35–42.

Opitz, M., & Guccione, L. (2009). *Comprehension and English language learners: 25 oral reading strategies that cross English language proficiency levels.* Portsmouth, NH: Heinemann.

Ovando, C. J., Collier, V. P., & Combs, M. C. (2005). *Bilingual and ESL classrooms: Teaching in multicultural contexts* (4th ed.). New York: McGraw-Hill Humanities.

Ovando, C. J., & Combs, M. C. (2011). *Bilingual and ESL classrooms: Teaching reading in multicultural contexts* (5th ed.). New York: McGraw-Hill Humanities.

Oxford, R. (1994, October). *Language learning strategies: An update.* Center for Applied Linguistics Online Resources: Digests. Retrieved from http://www .cal.org/resources/digest/oxford01.html

Pantaleo, S. (2004). Young children and radical change characteristics in picture books. *The Reading Teacher, 58*(2), 178–187.

Pearson, M. B. (2005). Speaking to their hearts: Using picture books in the history classroom. *Library Media Connection, 24*(3), 30–32.

Peregoy, S., & Boyle, O. (2005). *Reading, writing, and learning in ESL: A resource book for K–12 teachers* (4th ed.). Boston, MA: Pearson/Allyn & Bacon.

Petitto, L. (2003, December 4). *Revolutions in education and language.* Lecture for Office of English Language Acquisition, Washington DC. Retrieved from http://www.dartmouth.edu/~lpetitto/OELASummitTalk.pdf

Polette, K. (2005). *Read and write it out loud! Guided oral literacy strategies.* Boston, MA: Pearson.

Rasinski, T., & Padak, N. (2001). *From phonics to fluency: Effective teaching of decoding and reading fluency in the elementary school.* New York, NY: Longman.

Richard-Amato, P., & Snow, M. (2005). *Academic success for English language learners: Strategies for K–12 mainstream teachers.* White Plains, NY: Longman.

Rost, M. (2006). Areas of research that influence L2 instruction. In E. Uso–Juan & A. Martinez-Flor (Eds.), *Current trends in the development and teaching of the four language skills* (pp. 47–74). Berlin, Germany: Mouton.

Rothenberg, C., & Fisher, D. (2007). *Teaching English language learners: A differentiated approach.* Upper Saddle River, NJ: Pearson Education.

Russell, D. (2000). *Literature for children: A short introduction* (4th ed.). New York, NY: Longman.

Shak, J. (2006). Children using dictogloss to focus on form. *Journal of Reflections on English Language Teaching (RELT), 5*(2), 47–62.

Sipe, L. R. (1998). How picture books work: A semiotically framed theory of text-picture relationships. *Children's Literature in Education, 29*(2), 97–102.

Sipe, L. (2008). *Storytime: Young children's literary understanding in the classroom.* New York, NY: Teachers College Press.

Smallwood, B. A. (2002, November). *Thematic literature and curriculum for English language learners in early childhood education.* Center for Applied Linguistics online resources. Retrieved from http://www.cal.org/resources/digest/0208 smallwood.html

Smallwood, B. A., & Haynes, E. G. (2008). *Singable books: Sing and read your way to English proficiency.* Retrieved from http://www.cal.org/resources/digest/ singable.html

Tabors, P. O. (1997). *One child, two languages: A guide for preschool educators of children learning English as a second language.* Baltimore, MD: Paul H. Brookes.

Tiedt, I. (2000). *Teaching with picture books in the middle school.* Newark, DE: International Reading Association.

Tiedt, P., & Tiedt, I. (2005). *Multicultural teaching: A handbook of activities, information, and resources* (7th ed.). Boston, MA: Pearson/Allyn & Bacon.

Tompkins, G. (2006). *Literacy for the 21st century: A balanced approach* (4th ed.). Upper Saddle River, NJ: Pearson/Merrill Prentice-Hall.

Ulanoff, S., & Pucci, S. (1999). Learning words from books: The effects of read-aloud on second language vocabulary acquisition. *Bilingual Research Journal, 23*(4), 409–422.

Uribe, M., & Nathenson-Mejía, S. (2008). *Literacy essentials for English language learners: Successful transitions.* New York, NY: Teachers College Press.

Uso–Juan, E., & Martinez–Flor, A. (2006). Approaches to language learning and teaching: Toward acquiring communicative competence through the four skills. In E. Uso–Juan & A. Martinez–Flor (Eds.), *Current trends in the development and teaching of the four language skills* (1st ed., pp. 3–28). Berlin, Germany: Mouton De Gruyter.

Vacca J., Vacca, R., & Gove, M. (2012). *Reading & learning to read* (8th ed.). New York, NY: Harper Collins.

Van Zile, S., & Napoli, M. (2009). *Teaching literary elements with picture books: Engaging, standards–based lessons and strategies: Grades 4–8.* New York, NY: Scholastic Teaching Resources.

Weber, N. (2009). Pictures in our lives: Using wordless picture books with new language learners. In D. Meier (Ed.), *Here's the story: Using narrative to promote young children's language and literacy learning* (pp. 71–80). New York, NY: Teachers College Press.

Wiggins, G., & McTighe, J. (2005). *Understanding by design,* (expanded 2nd ed.). Upper Saddle River, NJ: Prentice-Hall.

Wiggins, G., & McTighe, J. (2011). *The understanding by design guide to creating high-quality units.* Alexandria, VA: Association for Supervision and Curriculum Development.

Wolfenbarger, C., & Sipe, L. (2007). A unique visual and literary art form: Recent research on picturebooks. *Language Arts, 83*(3), 273–280.

Yopp, H. K., & Yopp, R. H. (2006). *Literature–based reading activities* (4th ed.). Boston, MA: Allyn & Bacon.

Wong-Fillmore, L., & Snow, C. E. (2005). What teachers need to know about language, language proficiency, bilingualism, and academic achievement In R. Amato & M. A. Snow (Eds.), *Academic success for English language learners: Strategies for K–12 mainstream teachers* (pp. 47–75). White Plains, NY: Longman.

Index

CORWIN

A SAGE Company

The Corwin logo—a raven striding across an open book—represents the union of courage and learning. Corwin is committed to improving education for all learners by publishing books and other professional development resources for those serving the field of PreK–12 education. By providing practical, hands-on materials, Corwin continues to carry out the promise of its motto: **"Helping Educators Do Their Work Better."**